ROUTLEDGE LIBRARY EDITIONS: HIGHER EDUCATION

Volume 33

STATE GOVERNMENTS AND RESEARCH UNIVERSITIES

T0347444

STATE GOVERNMENTS AND RESEARCH UNIVERSITIES

A Framework for a Renewed Partnership

DAVID J. WEERTS

Routledge
Taylor & Francis Group

LONDON AND NEW YORK

First published in 2002 by RoutledgeFalmer

This edition first published in 2019
by Routledge
2 Park Square, Milton Park, Abingdon, Oxon OX14 4RN

and by Routledge
52 Vanderbilt Avenue, New York, NY 10017

Routledge is an imprint of the Taylor & Francis Group, an informa business

British Library Cataloguing in Publication Data
A catalogue record for this book is available from the British Library

ISBN: 978-1-138-32388-9 (Set)
ISBN: 978-0-429-43625-3 (Set) (ebk)
ISBN: 978-1-138-33091-7 (Volume 33) (hbk)
ISBN: 978-1-138-33095-5 (Volume 33) (pbk)
ISBN: 978-0-429-44751-8 (Volume 33) (ebk)

Publisher's Note
The publisher has gone to great lengths to ensure the quality of this reprint but points out that some imperfections in the original copies may be apparent.

Disclaimer
The publisher has made every effort to trace copyright holders and would welcome correspondence from those they have been unable to trace.

STATE GOVERNMENTS AND RESEARCH UNIVERSITIES
A Framework for a Renewed Partnership

David J. Weerts

ROUTLEDGEFALMER
NEW YORK & LONDON

Published in 2002 by
RoutledgeFalmer
29 West 35th Street
New York, NY 10001

Published in Great Britain by
RoutledgeFalmer
11 New Fetter Lane
London EC4P 4EE

RoutledgeFalmer is an imprint of the Taylor & Francis Group.

10 9 8 7 6 5 4 3 2 1

Library of Congress Cataloging-in-Publication Data

Weerts, David, 1971–
    State governments and research universities : a framework for a renewed partnership /
by David J. Weerts.
        p. cm. — (Higher education)
    Includes bibliographical references (p.) and index.
    ISBN 0-415-93247-5
    1. Higher education and state—United States—States. 2. Government aid to higher
education—United States—States. 3. Universities and colleges—Research—United
States—States. I. Title. II Higher education (Routledge (Firm))

LC173 .W44 2002
379.1'224'0973—dc21   2001049109

Printed on acid-free, 250 year-life paper
Manufactured in the United States of America

TABLE OF CONTENTS

List Of Tables

List Of Figures

Acknowledgments

I am deeply grateful for the many forms of support that have enabled me to complete this book. Tremendous thanks goes to my doctoral program advisor, Carolyn Kelley, who provided thoughtful feedback and guidance throughout the writing of my dissertation. In addition, Jacob Stampen, L. Allen Phelps, Clifton Conrad, and Donald Kettl graciously offered their expertise in higher education and public administration to help me frame the important questions covered in my analysis.

I am indebted to Donald Kettl and the Robert M. LaFollette School of Public Affairs at the University of Wisconsin-Madison for their financial assistance to support my dissertation research. A study of this scale would not have been possible without the fellowship support I received during the summer of 1998. I am honored and thankful to have received this assistance.

I am especially grateful for the wonderful support and love of my family. My parents, Les and Donna, continually offered their encouragement through cards, letters, phone calls, and visits to Madison. My siblings, Mark and Lynn, and their spouses, Christine and Nate, provided me with much needed fun and good humor.

Finally, this book is dedicated to the memory of my grandmother, Marion J. Smith, who loved her grandchildren and endlessly encouraged them to pursue their dreams. I continue to be blessed by the life lessons learned from Grandma Smith.

Abstract

A review of the literature suggests that higher education governance, institutional characteristics, and economic, demographic, political, and cultural factors play a critical role in determining state appropriations for public colleges and universities. Relying on these factors as a framework, this book examines the most compelling of these to understand differences in unrestricted state appropriations for Carnegie Public Research I Universities during the 1990s. By understanding these differences, a framework is advanced to underscore essential factors that play a critical role in promoting strong partnerships between state governments and research universities.

Both quantitative and qualitative methods were used in the study. First, regression analysis was employed to examine the impact of [the] twenty-six variables identified from the literature as important predictors of higher education appropriations. In the final regression model, three institutions were identified as representing [three] clear, but differing, levels of support: lower than predicted appropriations (Ohio State University), predicted appropriations (University of Wisconsin-Madison), and higher than predicted appropriations (University of Georgia).

A multi-case study design as described in Bogdan and Bicklen (1992) and Conrad, Howarth and Millar (1993) was used to learn about state support at these three institutions. The primary data collection method used was interviews targeting institutional leaders, state legislators, governing board officials, state administrators, and governor's staff in each state.

Institutional commitment to public service, strength of the higher education governance structure, and gubernatorial and legislative support emerged as critical elements accounting for differences in support between public research I universities. Specifically, that data shows that strong, recognizable outreach programs and structures are important to increasing the visibility of institutional service and consequently lead to greater state support. In addition, research I universities that are governed by a consolidated governing board are likely to have greater state appropriations compared to those in coordinating board systems because of governing boards' ability to mitigate competition between campuses. Finally, the support of the governor is among the most crucial factors that set the political stage and public disposition toward supporting higher education.

In sum, these findings suggest that institutional commitment to public service, a strong higher education governing body, and gubernatorial support are critical to promoting strong partnerships between state governments and research institutions. Throughout the book, these factors are examined through the lens of the organizational theory literature, suggesting a combination of rational, political, and cultural systems theories as most useful for understanding the organization, processes, and structures that explain key differences in state support for public research I universities. Most important, the theoretical framework offers ways in which state-institutional relations might be strengthened.

STATE GOVERNMENTS AND RESEARCH UNIVERSITIES

CHAPTER 1

Introduction and Overview

INTRODUCTION

The relationship between states and public colleges and universities is symbiotic: each depends on the other for survival. State governments play a critical role in financing higher education, while higher education institutions educate state residents and improve local economies. Still, most would concede that this relationship has been strained in recent years. A common measure pointing to this erosion between the state-university partnership is seen in the drastic cuts in appropriations for higher education during the past two decades. While state appropriations historically have been, and continue to be, the most important source of funds for all higher education (Gold, 1990), appropriations for post-secondary education have plummeted by more than 32 percent since 1979, adjusting for inflation (Mortenson, 1997).

The sources of higher education funding have shifted away from state appropriations toward private grants, gifts, student tuition and fees. Trend data from the University of Wisconsin System provides an example of how the landscape of higher education financing has changed dramatically. In FY 1973-74, Wisconsin general purpose revenue (GPR) accounted for 52 percent of funding for the UW system budget, while gifts, grants, and trust funds supplied 35 percent of the budget. Tuition and fees covered the remaining 13 percent of UW System expenses during that period. Today, the sources of higher education funding in Wisconsin look much different. In FY 1998-99, Wisconsin GPR accounts for only 33 percent of UW System expenses, whereas gifts, grants, and trust funds cover 50 percent. These statistics reveal that the primary burden of the expenses has virtually flip-flopped between the state and private or other sources. While not as dramatic, tuition and fees has also absorbed more of the costs at 17 percent in FY 1998-99 as opposed to 13 percent in FY 1973-74 (UW System Administration, 1999.)

State appropriations for the UW-Madison campus have similarly declined. In 1985-86, state support totaled 32.4 percent of the University's operating budget. In 1996-97, this support fell to 23.3 percent. It was during this fiscal year, that for the first time, total state dollars allocated to UW-Madison fell below the previous year's figure. Again, private sources and rising tuition have picked up the budget shortfall at the Madison campus. Development has especially emerged as a high priority. In 1998, gifts to the UW Foundation exceeded $108 million—a record gift year for the institution (University of Wisconsin Foundation, 1999).

There are many factors that explain the decline in state support, but most place the majority of the blame on the economic recession of the early 1980s and 1990s (Mortenson, 1997). Specifically, two major cuts between FY 1980-83 and FY 1990-94 contributed heavily to the slide in support for higher education. The drop during the 1990-91 fiscal year was especially formidable. During that period, 30 states cut their higher education budgets in the middle of the budget cycle—and for the first time in 33 years, the 1991-92 state budgets allotted less money to higher education than for the previous year (Schuh, 1993).

Drops in state support for discretionary programs such as higher education have also been attributed to a conservative shift in the federal government's role. During the last ten years, the federal government has transferred partial or full responsibility for many programs to the state and local level. This shift in philosophy known as "new federalism" has resulted in steep cuts in federal and state aid for municipal and county governments (Peterson, 1995). Not surprisingly, this shift has resulted in a significant squeeze in higher education appropriations for most states. The reason is that public universities are forced to more intensely compete for dollars with other state programs such as Medicaid, K-12 schools, social services, and corrections. Coupled with a struggling economy, this increased competition for resources accounts for the major reductions in higher education funding during the early-mid 1990s (Schuh, 1993).

If present trends continue, some analysts forecast a doomsday scenario for colleges and universities. A study conducted by a subsidiary of the RAND policy and research institute, suggests that the monetary difficulties of colleges and universities, once thought to be temporary, are part of long-term trends in the demand for enrollment and the supply of funding. The reason is that demand has increased sevenfold since World War II and is expected to continue growing over the next two decades. At the same time, operating costs have escalated and public-sector financial support has flattened (Commission on National Investment in Higher Education, 1997).

The study further suggests that the current trend in funding and the costs of higher education will mean a quadruple deficit in operating expenses for the nation's colleges and universities by 2015. Assuming tuition increases no faster than inflation, U.S. colleges and universities will fall $38 billion short of the annual budget they need to educate the student population expected in 2015 (Commission on National Investment in Higher Education, 1997).

While these long-term concerns prevail, it is important to note that some higher education institutions have enjoyed a recent boost in state appropriations thanks to a mid-1990s boom in the economy. The economy, which continued to be strong through 2000, is credited with promoting increases in many state university budgets during the late 1990s. An important statistic is that state appropriations for higher education increased an average of 9 percent during the 1996-97 fiscal year (Strang, Funk, Onofrio, 1997). The 1997-98 fiscal year showed similar growth, increasing higher education appropriations by 8 percent across the country (Grapevine, 1998).

But while the statistics reveal a national trend to revive, or at least sustain state support for higher education, there is a marked distinction between states during this period. While the majority of states have increased their support for higher education during the late 1990s, others have not made the same investment. For example, during FY 1996-97, six states actually decreased funding for higher education, whereas the others increased appropriations for their public colleges and universities.

The above discussion suggests that state support for higher education has been widely unstable during the past two decades and looks to be even shakier in the future. As the UW-Madison example demonstrates, the current relationship between state governments and the major public research campuses is especially tentative. New terms used to describe this relationship make this point. For example, it is widely known that many public research universities, including the University of Virginia, University of Michigan, and University of Wisconsin-Madison are now regarded as "state-assisted" as opposed to "state-supported" institutions (Ward, April 26, 1997). The switch from the label "supported" to "assisted" not only demonstrates these states' lessened financial commitment, but also suggests a significant shift in philosophy—that public research universities may not be wholly linked to their states as they once were.

This shift has had a strong effect on ways in which public institutions aim to compete and survive in the higher education marketplace. As already mentioned, one clear strategy is that public universities have concentrated more heavily on obtaining program revenue and private sources to maintain the quality of their academic programs in the absence of state dollars (Ward, April 26, 1997). In addition, many universities have turned to tightening enrollments and significantly increasing tuition as a way to remain competitive (Burke and Serban, 1998).

But many argue that the financial crisis is only one piece of the concern. The other is the drastic change in philosophy—that public research universities are beginning to look more like private research universities. Put simply, some fear that the public mission of the state research university is increasingly compromised and dwindling in importance. Land grant institutions in particular are viewed as losing their identity. A recent column written in the *Madison Capital Times* summed up one writer's concerns, "...our land grant system has largely been captured and derailed from its mission. Its publicly owned research facilities have become a sweet opportunity for those able to pay researchers and their graduate students—whether large corporations or national research funders whose agenda mirrors theirs" (Krome, 1999).

The National Association for State Universities and Land Grant Colleges (NASULGC) is addressing these issues through the work of the Kellogg Commission on the Future of State and Land-Grant Universities. Established in January 1996 with a grant from the Kellogg Foundation, the panel of university presidents is re-evaluating the way in which public universities interact with their states. The Commission has considered the funding crisis that faces public research universities and are beginning to address the impending critical question: how the downward trend in support will affect an institution's ability to effectively fulfill its public mission and what institutions might do to regain financial and public support (NASULGC, 1996).

As of May 1999, the Kellogg Commission has already tackled three of the five key issues identified as critical to regaining this support. Specifically, the commission has made recommendations and proposed possible solutions in improving the undergraduate student experience, ensuring access to higher education, and redefining outreach in the 21st century. The remaining topics to be explored are creating a learning society and reengineering the culture of the campus—a discussion about rethinking traditional reward systems (NASULGC, 1996). The Commission views these five areas as paramount in the pursuit of reconnecting universities with their states, and subsequently gaining financial support for higher education.

The study of state support for higher education is important because it addresses two critical issues: the survival of the public university and institutional commitment to the public university mission. As this introduction suggests, colleges and universities should be concerned about the future of state support and what it means for their prospect of long-term viability. While current economic conditions have promoted healthier budgets in recent years, the issue remains fundamental in the face of unforeseen changes in the market. The point is that long-term solutions must be formulated to encourage a healthier funding stream between states and their universities.

The second point is inextricably linked to the first. Public universities have a duty to reconnect with their states and will only earn the support of government officials if they successfully do so. Regaining state support relies on the integrity of institutions to return to their roots. National Association for State University and Land Grant College (NASULGC) President, Peter Magrath sums it up. Said Magrath, "Public universities must be financially stable and enjoy public confidence in order to perform their vital mission as the intellectual and educational service centers for America in the 21st century. But to earn this support, they must examine themselves . . . and then change and reform to better serve society" (Magrath, 1996). In sum, higher education institutions need the support of their states to survive, and an institution's commitment to its public role should be of paramount concern as it looks to strengthen its relationship with its state.

Among its most important contributions, the contents of this book place empirical evidence behind the assertion that future state support for research universities is contingent on an institution's ability to demonstrate its service to the state. The conclusions derived from the forthcoming statistical analysis and case studies reinforce the work of one panel of experts that declared, "Institutional reform is a prerequisite for increased public funding. Unless the higher education sector changes the way it operates . . . it will be difficult to garner the increases in public funding needed to meet future demands" (Commission of National Investment in Higher Education, 1997).

But beyond supporting the conventional calls for institutional reform, the book's case studies animate the importance of two partners critical to regaining support for research universities: higher education governing boards and state governments. The book illustrates the important role that governing boards play in defining the objectives of campuses, monitoring the accountability of institutions, and providing innovative leadership in state economic development. In addition, this analysis brings to life the importance of the partnership of the governor and the legislature to ensure the future vitality of higher education, and subsequently, the future economic health of the state.

PURPOSE OF THE STUDY

In order to advance a framework for strengthening partnerships between states and research universities, it is important to investigate factors that contribute to strong or weak relationships between these two entities. Such an analysis can provide significant clues about elements most essential to building strong state-institutional relationships.

As the introduction suggests, an important piece of evidence reflecting the strength of state-institutional relationships can be observed in the level of state appropriations that an institution receives from its state. While contextual differences exist between states and institutions that reflect varying levels of support across the country, such an analysis sheds light on conditions that promote strong or weak budgets for any institution.

To that end, this study seeks to identify and more deeply understand the factors that explain differences in state support for public research universities. Thus, the focus of this study is centered on understanding the differing conditions in states and institutions that vary significantly in their support of higher education. The primary goal of the analysis is identify and examine factors that promote strong funding streams between states and public universities. These themes derived from this analysis are woven together to provide a new framework for renewing the partnership between state governments and research universities.

Specifically, this study focuses on differences in state appropriations for public research universities during the 1990s. This study aims to accomplish three objectives: 1) Identify those factors which are the best predictors of state support for public universities; 2) Identify states that vary in their support of public higher education as a way to explore critical reasons behind their variations in appropriations; and 3) Learn about differences in institutional practices in states that vary in their support of higher education. Through successful fulfillment of these objectives, conclusions can be made about what factors are most important in building future partnerships between state governments and public research universities. These conclusions will be particularly useful for campus administrators as they seek to develop strategies to maximize state support for their institutions.

RESEARCH QUESTION AND DEFINITIONS

One all-encompassing question drives this study: what factors best explain the variation in state support for Public Research I Universities during the 1990s? Public Research I Universities are state institutions that offer a full range of baccalaureate programs, are committed to graduate education through the doctorate, give high priority to research, award 50 or more doctoral degrees each year, and receive annually $40 million or more in federal support. (Carnegie Foundation for the Advancement of Education, 1994).

"State support" in this study is defined as unrestricted state appropriations for higher education. Unrestricted appropriations are those state dollars used for higher education operating and research expenses. These expenses include, but are not limited to, faculty salaries, fringe benefits, wages, equipment, scholarships, and mandatory transfers. This definition excludes facilities budgets and exceptional units such as University Hospital and Clinics (IPEDS, 1998).

OUTLINE OF THE BOOK

This chapter has provided an introduction to the study and context for under-standing the issues surrounding a discussion of state support for higher education. Particular attention was paid to state funding trends and ideals that have been voiced in response these trends. Chapter two provides a literature review about what is known in the area of state support for public universities. In this chapter, organizational theory introducing rational, political, and cultural constructs are examined to identify possible predictors for state support of higher education. Together, the literature review and theoretical analysis provide the foundation, or conceptual framework, for the study.

Chapter three details the quantitative methods used to answer the research question, followed by the statistical findings and conclusions. Specifically, the chapter explains the use of the multiple regression analysis used to identify key predictors of state support for public research universities. The results of the variable testing are presented, offering the most compelling factors that emerged from the analysis. Furthermore, this chapter presents the methods of the qualitative analysis highlighting three case studies to follow: Ohio State University, University of Wisconsin-Madison, and the University of Georgia. The main themes that emerged from the case studies are presented in chapters four through six. In chapter seven, a cross-case analysis is provided as a way to animate the differences in the states and institutions studied.

Finally, chapter eight provides a new framework for renewing the partnership between state governments and research universities. To that end, the chapter summarizes conclusions based on both the quantitative and qualitative analysis and discusses implications for policy and strategy to apply what is learned. The conclusions are also used to bridge or fill in gaps as identified in the organizational theory analysis. The chapter ends with a discussion of the study's significance and offers avenues for future research.

CHAPTER 2

Understanding Factors that Influence State Support for Higher Education

Theoretical Orientations

A wide range of phenomena may explain differences in state support for colleges and universities. This chapter begins with an expansive discussion of the key elements that are known to play a role in state budgeting for higher education. Organizational theory is later introduced as a way to add depth of understanding to these factors. Together, the literature review and theoretical model provide a foundation for the conceptual framework in this study. This framework sets the stage for more focused attention on state support for the major research campuses—in particular, factors that are most important in determining levels of appropriations for public research I universities.

Two monographs provide the building blocks for the literature review. First, Dan Layzell and Jan Lyddon's work, *Budgeting for Higher Education at the State Level: Enigma, Paradox, and Ritual* (1990) provides a comprehensive overview of the complex environmental and internal processes involved in state budgeting for higher education. The monograph, constructed through a synthesis of literature related to higher education and state budgeting, is derived from publications in the fields of education, political science, public administration, and economics. In addition to more classic academic works, the authors used a variety of policy studies to inform their analysis.

Second, Edward Hines' piece, *Higher Education and State Governments: Renewed Partnership, Cooperation, or Competition?* (1988), provides an in-depth discussion about the relationship between public universities and their states, particularly during the 1980s. As Hines put it, the monograph "identifies policy issues in which states and higher education are involved, analyzes the relationship between government and higher education on the issues, and explores future directions in the evolving relationship between state governments and higher education" (Hines, 1988). Hines used classic works, unpublished reports, policy analyses, and doctoral dissertations to produce this report.

More contemporary works build on the two monographs as a way to voice recent contributions to the subject. In sum, the literature of the past two decades points to five major elements that determine the size and growth rate of higher education appropriations. These elements are economic and demographic factors, political influences, governance of higher education, state culture and education policy, and institutional characteristics and strategies.

ECONOMIC AND DEMOGRAPHIC VARIABLES

The literature suggests that the forecast or status of a state's economy significantly affects the rate of higher education funding in a particular state. Specifically, the unemployment rate, per capita income, availability of state revenues, and tax capacity help to determine the level at which the state will fund its public universities. Put simply, the overall wealth of a state is an important factor in determining the level of support for higher education (Layzell & Lyddon, 1990).

In addition, the composition of the population in a state is a factor that influences appropriations levels for colleges and universities. Changes in the overall population of the state, percentage of the population that are college age (18-24), and enrollment or participation rates are varying conditions that adjust the level of higher education funding over time (Layzell & Lyddon, 1990). Demographic information is critical when planning for the future of higher education and education in general. Demographic trend information can provide rational arguments for where states should invest in education in the future and can be used as a means to gain political support for certain types of programs (Blumenstyk, 1988).

Evidence of the power of economic and demographic factors as determinants of higher education appropriations is seen in the fact that support for higher education varied considerably among populous and wealthy regions during the mid-1980s. During that period, West Coast and New England states enjoyed a more prosperous economy, resulting in greater appropriations for higher education. Also, support for higher education increased in the sun-belt states due to a surge in population growth in these areas. In contrast, the Midwest experienced an "out-migration" of residents, and some states, such as Ohio and Indiana, struggled to make the transition from an industrial to service economy. These factors explained much of the variation in state higher education funding during that period (Layzell and Lyddon,1990).

Beyond issues of state wealth and population, the symbiotic relationship between higher education and economic growth is known to be important. Linking higher education to a state's economy positively affects the level of higher education funding in a particular state primarily because investing in universities is considered one means of improving a state's economy. During the late 1980s, states with large increases in appropriations for higher education explicitly linked higher education with economic development in that state. These states invested more heavily in higher education because it was considered a means to improve tax capacity (Hines, Hickrod, Pruyne, 1989).

An example investment in higher education as a mechanism to stimulate the economy can be seen in the Ben Franklin Partnership program in Southeastern Pennsylvania. Established in the early 1980s, the economic development project was formed in response to a loss of 175,000 manufacturing jobs in the state. Pennsylvania has four universities among the top 50 graduate universities nationwide and produced among the largest group of engineers in the country. Using the strength of these universities, the State made a commitment to provide challenge grants to university-based projects funded by businesses. In a four-year period, the program attracted $61.4 million dollars in private venture capital. Because of its success, the Ben Franklin Technology Center of Southeastern Pennsylvania continues to receive generous levels of financial support from the Commonwealth General Assembly (Pennsylvania's Ben Franklin Partnership, 1999).

As the Pennsylvania example demonstrates, investment in higher education economic initiatives is an important mechanism that some states use to invigorate the economy. Because of the clear benefits to the state, public universities that become more involved with improving the state economic base are most likely to accrue more benefits (Layzell and Lyddon, 1990).

POLITICAL FACTORS

State Politics and the Budget

The political influences surrounding higher education appropriations come to life primarily during state budgetary debates. Budgetary control is a crucial piece of the puzzle and involves "conflict among people who want different outcomes and who attempt to exert power in order to make the size and distribution of spending different than it might otherwise have been." (Wildavsky, 1992). The legislature and governor are the ultimate players in the budget creation process and set the stage for the investment in government services and programs.

Because of variations in constitutional power among states, one can not make general assumptions about the power of governors across the county. However, it is clear that the governor's role in higher education has become extremely important in the last two decades. It was during the 1980s that governors emerged as visible, active policy makers with significant influence on post-secondary education. In fact, Hines (1988) argues that they have become the single most important person in higher education in many states. Beyond budgetary power, governors approve or veto appropriations bills and fiscal legislation important to higher education and many operate bureaus that review operating budgets for university systems (Hines, 1988).

In recent years, governors have become more vocal than ever about their agenda and role in planning for higher education in their states. In a 1998 survey conducted by the Education Commission on the States, governors viewed themselves as bearing the primary responsibility for bringing about needed changes in the direction of state-college systems. The governors called for fundamental changes in the institution's policies and practices so that, among other changes, faculty research becomes more directly tied to state needs. Issues such as tenure and faculty service to the state are among recent concerns of U.S. governors.

Considering these examples, it is clear that accountability is an important factor as governors consider investing in colleges and universities (Schmidt, 1998).

While the role of governors has evolved, so too have state legislatures. Since the 1950s, legislators have become more active and informed on all issues including higher education (Hines, 1988). In a recent survey by the National Education Association (NEA), state legislators regarded themselves as more "action-oriented" than their predecessors when it came to higher education (Ruppurt, 1997). But at the same time, legislators of both parties express concerns about the adverse effect of tax reform and other cost cutting measures on the state's investment in higher education. In addition, other state priorities have taken precedent during the 1990s. For instance, state governments have taken a tougher stance on crime which has inadvertently resulted in diminishing support for discretionary programs like higher education. A clear example is in California. During the early 1990s higher education funding in that state declined by 25 percent while corrections grew by the same amount. Beyond prisons, property tax relief has become an important issue with many states shouldering more responsibility for funding elementary and secondary education. It is also important to note that Medicaid costs have surpassed higher education as the second largest outlay for state budgets (Ruppurt, 1997).

Like the governors, legislators have their share of concerns about efficiency and accountability issues in regard to public colleges and universities. Faculty workload and time-to-degree studies suggest that institution's stewardship to taxpayers is poor (Ewell, 1994). Some higher education analysts are concerned about the impact this has on the future of self-regulation in public universities. Peter Ewell of National Center for Higher Education Management Systems summed it up, "The problem has always been much more a 'crisis of confidence' rooted in a conviction that higher education is managed haphazardly and has increasingly been unable to regulate itself effectively" (Ewell, 1994 p. 25). It is reasonable to suggest that these concerns can have an affect on the level of state support for colleges and universities.

Federalism and Its Effect on State Spending for Higher Education

The federal government's role is important to consider when reviewing state budgets for higher education. Chapter one briefly pointed out that the mid-1980's introduced a new form of federalism that affected levels of appropriations for higher education in many states. During that time, the mood became one of deregulation and decentralization resulting in annual federal cuts in student aid, including Pell grants and student loans. The effects of federal conservatism had far-reaching ramifications for state lawmakers and their subsequent support for higher education (Schuh, 1993).

First, states were unable to increase support because federal funds were cut, shifting costs to students in the form of higher tuition and reducing programs as a way to cut costs (Schuh, 1993). Second, deregulation meant that partial or full responsibility for many programs were transferred from the federal to state and local level. Municipal and county governments especially suffered steep cuts in federal and state aid in the late 1980s and along with the cuts, new federal demands forced states to expand their entitlements, further increasing the burden on state budgets. California's Medicaid program grew at double-digit rates during the early 1990s, in part because the federal government was asking California, and other states, to expand the number of services covered by the program (Peterson, 1995).

This shift in federal control resulted in a significant squeeze in higher education appropriations for most states because public universities were forced to more intensely compete for dollars with other state programs (Schuh, 1993). The point is that politics at the federal level has had an effect on state legislator's reaction to balancing the competing needs of the state. Because of the shift towards deregulation, legislators will be addressing a far wider range and complex set of issues than ever before (Ruppurt, 1997).

GOVERNANCE AND BUDGETING FORMULAS

Higher education governance and authority are important to consider when discussing state support for higher education. Two authority structures dominate at this time: governing boards and coordinating boards (MacTaggart, 1996). Governing boards have authority not found in coordinating boards in three areas: authority over how individual campuses are governed, authority over the internal affairs of campuses, and authority over how campus budgets are carried out. Coordinating boards do not govern institutions, rather they focus on state and system needs and priorities. Essentially, these boards aim to plan for state postsecondary education as a whole but do not have authority over the campuses (McGuinness, 1997).

One disadvantage of governing boards is that they are seen as being more closely aligned with the campuses than with state officials. This may not ingratiate governing boards with governors and legislators. However, they have better control over institutional matters which is argued to be best handled by a more hierarchical structure (Hines, 1988). Coordinating boards, on the other hand, have a weaker but broader scope of authority than governing boards. They are said to relate better to legislators and the private sector and tend not to get as engulfed in campus matters as their governing board counterpart. One disadvantage however is the board's lack of influence over a campus resulting in campus governing boards and presidents acting on their own in inappropriate times. In these situations, campus presidents and boards may show little concern for the coordinating board or other institutions in the state (Hines, 1988). These "end-runs" may place strain on relationships and cause instability in funding streams among institutions.

At present 23 of the 50 states are run by consolidated governing boards, and 21 states operated coordinating regulatory boards. Six states and Washington D.C. use a planning agency to direct the activities of the institutions. These agencies have little authority beyond voluntary planning and convening role to ensure good communications among institutions and sectors (McGuinness, 1997).

The literature suggests that variations in state appropriations among governance structures lie in whether campuses are in multi-campus systems or consolidated systems of higher education. Multi-campus systems are those systems distinguishable by the "home" institution being the oldest and largest, accompanied by two or four-year branch campuses and specialized institutions, such as a medical school, all governed by a single board (Hines, 1988). Pennsylvania State University is an example of a multi-campus system. Consolidated systems, on the other hand, include campuses that existed before the system was created. These institutions are often located at great distances from each other and administrated separately. The governing boards, developed after the campuses were merged, are often located in the state capital (Hines, 1988). The University of Wisconsin System is an example of a consolidated system of higher education.

Specifically, it is known that multi-campus universities showed a slightly stronger rate of gain in state support than consolidated systems prior to 1986. However, in 1986, the rates of gain in the two types of systems were identical, and beginning in 1987 and continuing in 1988, the rates of gain in consolidated systems began to outdistance the rates of gain in multi-campus universities. Hines (1988) theorizes that reasons for these differences are political rather than based on objective measures, such as the budget base or revenue patterns.

Within a particular governance system, funding formulas including performance-based funding may affect the level of higher education appropriations for a campus. Funding formulas refer to a mathematical basis for allocating dollars to institutions of higher education using rations, rates, and percentages derived from cost studies and peer analyses (McKeown and Layzell, 1994). Formulas are used as a means of achieving a sense of adequacy, stability, and predictability in institutional funding levels—established to distribute public funds for higher education in a rational and equitable manner. However, funding formulas have evolved over time into complicated methods with multiple purposes and outcomes. In a survey conducted in 1994, seven state university systems indicated that they used a funding formula, 13 said they use an incremental formula for funding, and 17 use a combination of formula and incremental budgeting (McKeown and Layzell, 1994).

Total quality management has gained consideration as state officials struggle to define measures of "quality" (McKeown and Layzell, 1994). Thus, performance-based funding and budgeting emerged in the call for more accountability and the desire to align universities more closely with state definitions of quality. Performance *funding* ties special sums directly to results of specific indicators. Performance *budgeting* considers results of performance indicators as a factor in the total funding of colleges and universities. In essence, performance based indicators shift the focus from what states should do for their colleges toward what colleges should do for their states. Currently, ten states have performance-based funding and eight states have performance-based budgeting (Burke and Serban, 1997).

Governing or coordinating boards often have a role in selecting the indicators to be used for the funding formula (Burke and Serban, 1997). Because the success or failure of meeting the objectives in performance-based funded or budgeted states can have a significant affect on appropriations for these institutions, campus administrators are beginning to implement Continuous Quality Indicators (CQI). Works by Lee and Smith (1994) and Seymour and Associates (1996) are guiding administrators as they integrate the concept of "quality" in a higher education setting (Fenske and Stampen, 1997).

STATE CULTURE

To study culture, one must study systems of meaning because "systems of meaning constitute culture" (Marshall, Mitchell, Wirt, 1989). An analysis of a state's culture can help one understand the meaning behind structure, formal offices and rules, processes for gaining power, and behaviors and attitudes of state policy-makers. A cultural paradigm is grounded in two central premises: that culture shapes institutions and traditions, and culture is reflected in written and unwritten codes of behavior (Marshall, Mitchell, Wirt, 1989).

Applied to a discussion about higher education appropriations, these authors would suggest that an examination of culture is essential to understanding budgetary outcomes. This is because new statutes and budgets are ultimately the concrete outcomes of values transformed into policy (Marshall, Mitchell, Wirt, 1989).

Broadly speaking, historical, religious, social, and ethnic values define a states overall culture. Tradition is also an important factor that shapes a state culture as it relates to educational policy in a state (Marshall, Mitchell, Wirt, 1989). Wisconsin provides a compelling example of how history and tradition provide the touchstone for the direction of higher education in this State. The University of Wisconsin became famous for its early 20th century commitment to applying the expertise of the academy to the common people of the State. In 1911, President Charles Van Hise stated that the underlying philosophy of the idea was "the placing of the expert knowledge of the few to the service of all." Working with UW faculty and administration, Governor Robert M. LaFollette used the University of Wisconsin as an instrument to solve the social and economic problems of the day (Berry, 1972).

This precedent set forth by LaFollette and Van Hise provided the bedrock for the outreach and public service values found in Wisconsin's higher education culture. The power of the Wisconsin Idea concept is still evident as UW administrators look to update it for the 21st Century. In fact, the Wisconsin Idea warrants an important piece in UW-Madison's "Vision for the Future" (Ward, 1999) and has been revitalized as the institution celebrates its sesquicentennial. A recent policy report stated the importance of the concept arguing that "Without a strong Wisconsin Idea, our state will be unable to rise to its challenges..." (Kettl, 1999).

Beyond these examples, historical precedents may shape culture in other ways. For instance, the strength and numbers of private universities in a particular state may affect citizens' feelings toward public higher education (Layzell and Lyddon, 1990). In states with historically strong private schools, legislators may feel less pressure to invest in state institutions. In particular, this may be true in the northeastern states where they have developed "systems" of higher education that include heavy reliance on private institutions. Meanwhile, the rest of the states have concentrated on developing diverse public institutions to meet the varying needs of citizens (McKeown and Layzell, 1994). Thus, this private school factor may make a difference when legislators determine budgets for public institutions.

When speaking of cultures it is also appropriate to discuss public attitudes that sway legislators' support for higher education. Taxpayers in recent years have been described as a "fiercely anti-tax, anti-spending public that is skeptical about the ability of government to solve its problems" (Ruppert, 1997). The public view of higher education has taken a downturn as studies confirm that many Americans believe that a college education is too expensive and that mismanagement and overpaid administrators are to blame. Media attention to scandals involved with misuse of federal money and unemployed graduates compounds the belief that higher education is in disarray (MacTaggart, 1996). These stories and myths create a culture where taxpayers are soured toward investment in public programs including higher education. Cultural factors, thus, can reasonably have a strong impact on governors and legislators' decisions to invest in colleges and universities.

INSTITUTIONAL CHARACTERISTICS AND STRATEGIES

The aforementioned factors touch on the broad influences affecting state support for all higher education institutions in a particular state. Focusing on research I campuses, this study hypothesizes that characteristics of a particular institution may also have a strong impact on the level of appropriations for a research I campus. These characteristics include total enrollment of undergraduate and graduate students, tuition and fees revenue, total federal grants and contracts, and total private gifts and grants. Where the university spends its money may also make a difference in how well the state supports that particular institution's mission. For example, a state may accord a higher value on one institutional goal than another, thereby basing the size of the university budget on how well the institution advances this piece of its mission. In addition, the campus attention to accountability, quality, and access might affect how states respond to particular institutions. In other words, the success of campus stewardship for public higher education goals might have an impact on how well they are supported.

Institutional characteristics have an effect in less obvious ways. The visibility of a particular campus can make a difference. In particular, a correlation exists between institutions with successful athletic teams and increases in state support (Layzell and Lyddon, 1990). The theory is that a winning team increases the visibility of an institution, thereby resulting in greater public and legislative interest in the campus.

Institutional strategies and lobbying efforts have been known to influence the levels of support campuses receive from their states. State lobbying for higher education has grown significantly during the last twenty-five years and have focused on key ingredients: establishing trust with legislators, providing accurate and reliable information, maximizing communications among law makers and educators, and building coalitions. During the mid-1980s, Texas campuses increased lobbying markedly and higher education became better represented by powerful allies external to the academy. Business leaders and the lieutenant governor formed a political action committee called "Grassroots Texas" to put higher education on the forefront of the political agenda. Participants in the effort traveled the state, talking about their willingness to pay higher taxes and the role of colleges in improving the state's economy. An increase in state support for Texas institutions during that period was credited to this effort (Hines,1988).

More recently public institutions in Virginia benefited immensely from the help of a political action group working on behalf of higher education needs. From 1995-1997, the Virginia Business Council played a prominent role in increasing support for public institutions in the Commonwealth. The Council, which includes more than 40 top executives of Virginia's largest companies as well as the presidents of its leading colleges and universities, was credited in bringing about these changes: 1) state spending on higher education increased by $230 million from 1995-1997; 2) a tax cut proposal by Republican Governor George Allen was defeated, after business leaders testified against it; 3) Council members helped to elect state legislative candidates who were supportive of higher education and to defeat some who were not. It has been reported that the Business Higher Education Partnership in Florida has also had positive results (Trombley, 1997).

Campuses continue to increase their exposure as a way to demonstrate the institution's benefit and worthiness of investment. The University of North Carolina-Chapel Hill, for example, initiated the practice of "On the Road" events designed to heighten the visibility of the institution in rural areas of the State. This event showcases the talents of professors and their service to state residents. The University of Wisconsin-Madison is one of many other institutions that have adopted this practice.

LITERATURE REVIEW FRAMEWORK

The multi-faceted factors identified in this chapter might be easily lost in a strictly narrative form. To better visualize these factors a "fishbone diagram" or "cause and effect" diagram is employed in this study. A fishbone diagram graphically maps out factors or characteristics thought to affect a problem or desired outcome. Such a diagram is useful because is makes the relationships among factors visible, providing a structured format for documenting verified causal relationships (Scholtes, 1994).

In Figure 2:1, the fishbone diagram helps to organize the literature review surrounding the research problem. Thus, the "head" of the diagram is a description of the general concept in this study—factors known to play a role in higher education budgeting. Each of the "bones" represent the general influences that are key to understanding state support for higher education. Finally, the smaller "bones" represent deeper influences within the family of these of general factors.

ORGANIZATIONAL THEORY

While the fishbone diagram illustrates the breadth of factors involved in determining state support for colleges and universities, organizational theory is used in this study to add depth of understanding to these factors. A review of organizational theory is compelling because higher education institutions and states are managed through a series of organizational structures and social processes. State budgeting decisions are also filtered through these organizational means. An organizational analysis promotes a more thorough understanding of these processes as a way to learn about their underlying influence in the budgeting process. For these reasons, organizational theory enriches the conceptual framework in this study, adding theoretical support for the key factors identified in the literature.

As a discipline, the study of organizations is one of the most vigorous areas in the social sciences, encompassing a number of theories and competing approaches to explain a vast array of organizational phenomenon (Scott, 1992). Within these approaches are three widely recognized levels of analysis. The first investigates organizational life at a micro level—investigating how individual behaviors and attitudes affect an organization and its outcomes. The intermediate level explores structures, divisions, and social processes as a way to characterize organizations and organizational behaviors. The third level is a macro look at the organization, focusing on organizations as independent actors functioning in a larger system of complex relationships (Scott, 1992).

Borrowing from these general concepts, organizational theory will be divided into two levels in this study: the state level and the institutional level. The state level covers a macro perspective. A look through this wider lens helps conceptualize the complex relationships within the larger state policy environment. In other words, it demonstrates how higher education fits into the broader framework of state policy. On the institutional level, higher education budgeting differences will be viewed through the activities of the research universities themselves, examining how state and higher education structures and social processes affect support for particular institutions. On this plane, campus behaviors and attitudes affecting state support for these institutions are considered.

THEORETICAL ORIENTATIONS

These levels are further understood through an examination of various theoretical orientations. Organizational theorists have employed numerous orientations or metaphors advancing diverse ways of thinking about organizations. For example, some theorists see organizations as "organisms"—the premise that organizations are born, grow and develop as various species over time. In another perspective, organizations as "brains" focuses on organizations in terms of information processing, learning and intelligence. Yet another view is that organizations are "psychic prisons," entrapping individual thoughts, fears, ideas, and beliefs as ways that organizations are self-perpetuating (Morgan, 1986).

This study relies on more conventional lenses to view state and higher education organizations. In particular, rational, political, and cultural systems

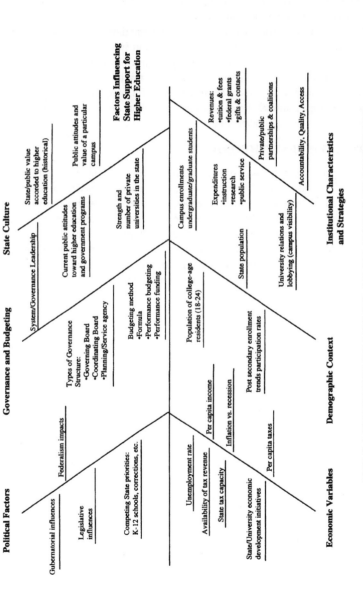

FIG 2:1 FISHBONE DIAGRAM: LITERATURE FRAMEWORK

theories are advanced as the theoretical bedrock of the preceding literature review. These three perspectives are used because the literature review most clearly supports these perspectives. The following section will demonstrate the usefulness of application to these orientations. The goal is to weave the theoretical constructs into an analysis of the supporting literature.

Finally, the purpose of this analysis is to examine whether any of these theories are ultimately most compelling to explain variations in state support for research universities. In other words, this study intends to learn whether the following theories or combination thereof, can be useful as a way to interpret my findings or conclusions. The intent is that the analysis will fill in gaps or build bridges between these organizational theories as they contribute to an understanding of state support for research I universities.

RATIONAL SYSTEMS THEORIES

The rational perspective discusses organizations in terms of being mechanical and "data-driven." In this perspective, organizations are viewed as machines designed to achieve predetermined goals and objectives, organized in a way that promotes optimal efficiency (Morgan, 1986). Data is used to determine levels of resources needed to keep these machines working. The literature review points out that legislators use rational measures, such as economic and demographic data, to make decisions about higher education budgeting. In addition, campuses employing rational strategies maximize their appropriations. Two rational theories make this clear.

Rational Choice and Bounded Rationality Theory

Rational choice and bounded rationality suggest that optimal decisions are made based on an objective review of data and investigation of alternative choices. In this perspective, decision-making can be analyzed in terms of variables that affect organizational goals; variables that affect organizational expectations and choice (Cyert and March, 1963). As was discussed, many of the factors that affect higher education spending—taxable resources and population density included—are economic and demographic variables. These variables may easily be classified as rational because they are based on objective measures of current and forecasted conditions in a state. Based on this fact, some analyst have concluded that government expenditure is determined by more rational forces than political ones (Peterson, 1995). Thus, an application of rational choice theory is relevant to understanding higher education budgets, and the extent to which policy makers support higher education based on an objective view of data.

Competitive Strategy Theory

Competitive strategy advances the explanation that organizational leaders choose optimum strategies to compete with other resource dependent entities given regulators, competitors, and barriers (Child, 1973). In this view, organizations are driven to incorporate the practices and procedures defined by prevailing rationalized concepts of organizational work that are institutionalized in society. Organizations that incorporate these practices increase their legitimacy and survival prospects (Meyer and Rowan, 1977). The theory would suggest that campus administrators create rational structures and pursue rational activities to accomplish higher education goals. This is done as a way to survive among competitors. Examples might include having visible structures in place to advance the institution's research, instruction, and public service mission. Since efficiency and costs are prevailing concepts among the public, attention to accountability is another rational strategy that institutional leaders employ to legitimize their operations.

POLITICAL SYSTEMS THEORIES

Higher education budgeting can be easily viewed through a political lens, focusing on the relationships between interests, conflict, and power. Organizational politics arise when people think differently and want to act differently, creating a tension that must be resolved through political means (Morgan, 1986). Three political theories are particularly relevant in a review of higher education budgeting decisions. These theories address individual and institutional powers that push and pull in the higher education policy environment, as well as coalitions that exert power and determine higher education's place on the agenda. This perspective might label higher education budgeting decisions as "power-driven."

Strategic Contingency Theory

Strategic contingency theory suggests that the course of an organization will be determined by power actors, or groups of power holders, that best manage uncertainty in an organization (Scott, 1992). Uncertainty can be defined as a lack of information about future events, so that alternatives and their outcomes are unpredictable. Actors that are most likely to best manage this uncertainty are those who are difficult to substitute and are central to many of the activities in the organization (Hickson, Hinings, Lee, Schneck, Pennings, 1977). Simply put, the theory suggests that organizations often depend on the influence of powerful actors who are critical to determining an institution's fate. An application of this theory to higher education budgeting suggests the importance of key leaders in the higher education environment. In particular, the interaction of the system president, key legislators, and the governor gives power to those who are central to setting the future agenda for higher education in a state. The higher education governance structure itself is another key player that exerts power in this arena. It is known that the governance structure has various degrees of power to manage the critical events of universities within the state.

Resource Dependency Theory

The central premise of resource dependency is that an organization needs to extract resources from the environment to survive and in effect, place other competing organizations into external dependencies. Organizations, therefore, pursue political strategies that will enhance their bargaining position among other dependent agencies. How important and how scarce these resources and determine the nature and the extent of dependency (Pfeffer and Salancik, 1978). The resource dependency approach is similar to the strategic contingency perspective, but its primary focus is the organization itself, its behavior and its relations with organizations, rather than its individual units (Scott, 1992). A fitting example of resource dependency in higher education might be seen in the effects of "new" federalism described earlier in this chapter. Federal deregulation has magnified the power struggle between state organizations; particularly between higher education, K-12 schools, corrections, and health care. The effect is that higher education has struggled to compete with these entities and has been forced into an external dependency. Resource dependency may be a useful way to explain variations in higher education funding, depending on the variation of competition and priorities within a particular state.

Interpreted another way, a resource dependency perspective could be used to discuss political pulls with the higher education governance structure. As the literature review pointed out, the governance structure can be a powerful actor, central in campus administration, having the power to manage important events. Depending on governance authority, institutions may have the ability to place other campuses into competing dependencies. In other words, competition for resources may vary in intensity between campuses depending on the strength of the higher education governance structure in a particular state. For example, stronger governance systems may have more coordination and control over the lobby activities of campuses than weaker systems.

Coalition Building

Coalitions are subsets of individuals and groups that share consensual goals and work toward a common end (Cyert and March, 1963). Often, organizations form coalitions for the purpose of accruing mutual benefits. In some coalition arrangements, the primary focus is on influencing the distribution of resources to organizational members. These types of coalitions are called distributive coalitions (Scott, 1992). Colleges and universities are examples of organizations that create distributive coalitions or partnership initiatives as a means of gaining funding leverage to advance common goals. As was pointed out in the literature review, the business and higher education community in Virginia successfully locked arms in support of post-secondary education for the purpose of economic growth and maintenance of an educated citizenry. In addition, increases in higher education appropriations during the early 1980s were directed toward campuses that partnered with the private sector (Johnson, 1984). Coalition-building theory merits consideration as it is used to understand the power of collaboration in the public policy arena.

CULTURAL SYSTEMS THEORIES

A third point of analysis in this study is the cultural perspective. Morgan (1986) notes that cultural symbols and rituals, attitudes, opinion, and general conditions shape organizational reality. A study of organizational culture helps to explain some of the more incomprehensible and irrational aspects of groups and organizations. The emphasis of this analysis is the shared, taken-for-granted basic assumptions held by the members of the group or organization (Schein, 1992). Layzell and Lyddon (1990) pointed out that state culture has an important impact on the extent to which a state supports higher education. In this perspective, higher education budgeting decisions might be labeled as "values/symbols driven." Four theories are advanced to explain the importance of culture in the higher education budgeting environment.

Obligatory Action and Enactment Theory

Obligatory action and enactment theory are quite similar. Obligatory action suggests that behavior can be viewed as contractual implicit agreements to act appropriately in return for being treated appropriately. Unlike decision-making in a rational perspective, obligatory action is grounded in cultural norms—the criterion being appropriateness rather than consequential optimality (March, 1981). Instead of contemplating alternatives, values and consequences, the decision-maker asks, 'what kind of situation is this?' what kind of person am I?' and "what is appropriate for me to do in a situation like this?" (March, 1981). In higher education budgeting decisions, the theory would suggests that some state legislators might decide to increase support for higher education simply based on a general feeling that it is an appropriate action or that it is their role to do so, not based on rational or established criteria.

Similarly, enactment theory suggests that decisions are driven by assumptions of "how things need to be" or by general perceptions of what is happening. In essence, the model theorizes that values and goals are manipulated or shaped organizationally and are then ultimately expressed as givens. In other words, a paradigm is developed over time and eventually embedded within the general belief systems of decision-makers or the public at large (Suchman, 1996). Accordingly, it is known that support for universities is, in part, driven by public attitudes, perceptions, or historical assumptions of "how things should be." (Layzell and Lyddon, 1990). These cultural theories have merit because citizens' collective value accorded to higher education is a known factor in determining the level of support for higher education in a given state.

Symbolic Decision-Making Theory

Symbolic decision-making theory suggests that a powerful actor reinforces or promotes a value through specific actions, and complementing language and symbols supporting that particular action and value. This use of symbols and action serves to legitimize and rationalize organizational decisions and policies. Symbolic decisions construct or maintain belief systems which assure continued compliance, commitment, and positive affect on the part of participants (Pfeffer, 1981). Schein (1992) speaks of these actions as ways that "cultural managers" can effectively influence organizations. Especially in growing organizations, successful cultural managers externalize their own assumptions and embed them consistently in the mission goals and structures and working procedures (Schein, 1992). Symbolic decision-making can be observed in the state budgeting process. In particular, governors' and legislators make symbolic decisions to send the public a message about their support for various initiatives and programs. This action may be conducted as a way to reinforce strongly held values or embed new ones into the state culture.

Institutional Theory

Institutional theorists contend that changes in organizational structures and messages can serve as an important signaling mechanism to the organization's constituencies about the values of an organization. Institutional theory emphasizes that organizations are open systems that are strongly influenced by their environments—but that many of these forces are not the result of rational pressures for more effective performance, but of social and cultural pressures to conform to conventional beliefs. (Scott, 1992). Meyer and Rowan (1977) argue that that formal structures of organizations have meaning and importance regardless of whether they affect the behaviors of performers in the technical core, but that they effectively symbolize meaning and order. Organizations that do this maximize their legitimacy and increase their resources and survival capabilities (Meyer and Rowan, 1977).

For example, Scott (1992) says that an office for affirmative action can signal to interested parties an organizations commitment to the goals of this program independently of whether or not affirmative action policies are pursued. Such signals are taken seriously by outsiders because changes in structure are highly observable and consume resources unlike pronouncements of goals or policies, which are relatively inexpensive. In the same way, higher education institutions create structures to maintain favorable perceptions among the public and legislators. This is done as a way to secure a prominent social position within the state culture. Public service units and affirmative action offices might be examples of structures specifically set up to send a message about the values advanced at the institution, regardless of their success in realizing these goals.

THEORETICAL FRAMEWORK

Table 2:1 illustrates the linkages between the literature and these supporting organizational theories and perspectives. As the table demonstrates, theories from these three perspectives can be used, in part, to understand those factors which affect higher education budgeting decisions within a state.

The fishbone diagram and theoretical framework provide the touchstone for the remainder of this study. As Chapter three points out, the methods used to answer the research question are anchored in this framework. This chapter will describe this relationship more in-depth.

Table 2:1. Organizational Theory Framework

	Rational Perspective "Data Driven"	Political Perspective "Power Driven"	Cultural Perspective "Values/Symbols Driven"

State Level	Rational Choice and Bounded Rationality
	Economic:
	• unemployment rate
	• availability of tax revenue
	• state tax capacity
	• per capita income
	• inflation vs. recession
	• per capita taxes
	• state/university economic development initiatives
	
	Demographic
	• State population
	• Population of college-age residents (18-24)
	• Post-secondary enrollment trends/participation rates
		Strategic Contingency
		• Gubernatorial influences
		• Legislative influences
		• System/Governance leadership
		
		Resource Dependency
		• Federalism impacts
		• Competing State Priorities
		  • K-12 education
		  • Corrections
		  • Health care
		• Type of governance structure and budgeting methods (competition between campuses)
			Enactment/Obligatory Action
			• State/public value accorded to higher education (historical)
			• Public attitudes/value of a particular campus
			• Current attitudes toward higher education and government spending
			• Strength and number of private universities in the state
			
			Symbolic Decision-Making
			• Gubernatorial support
			• Legislative support (based on perceived value of institution or higher education in general)

Institutional Level	Competitive Strategy Institutional strategies and structures • Accountability • Quality • Access/Outreach • Revenues/Expenditures/Enrollments	Coalition Building • Private/public coalitions and partnerships • Political alliances	Institutional Theory • University relations and lobbying • Campus visibility • Structures to promote campus

CHAPTER 3

Mixed Method Design and Analysis

SEQUENTIAL MIXED METHOD DESIGN

Many scholars including Eisner (1981), Firestone (1987), and Howe (1988) point out the virtues of using a variety of methods—both quantitative and qualitative—to gain an understanding about various phenomenon. These scholars argue that the diversity of approaches allows one to better know and understand different things about the world (Glesne and Peshkin, 1992).

Recognizing the legitimacy of using multiple approaches, the methods of this study are founded on the sequential mixed method design as defined by Tashakkori and Teddlie (1998). The authors' explain that the approach involves employing both quantitative and qualitative in two distinct phases of a study: a quantitative phase and then a qualitative phase, or vice versa. One purpose of the sequential method is to use the results from the first method to inform the use of the second method (Greene, Caracelli, Graham 1989). In my analysis, I draw on the results from a regression analysis to build a multi-case study. Upon completion of the case studies, I triangulate the findings with the regression model to form my overall conclusions.

Answering the research question in this study is best served by using both quantitative and qualitative methods. A brief application of both modes of inquiry makes this point. First, the quantitative approach in this study focuses on identification of variables (and whether they are statistically significant) to make informed judgments about factors most important to explaining differences in state support for research universities. While using statistical evidence to understand the relative strength of these factors is a compelling way to formulate conclusions, the literature review in chapter two pointed out that these elements are not so precisely measured. A qualitative approach is useful then, because it is grounded in the premise that variables are complex, interwoven, and difficult to measure (Glesne and Peshkin, 1992).

To that end, my analysis relies on the duality of approaches to make informed conclusions in response to the research question. Specifically, this study begins with a regression model incorporating the variables identified in the literature as being critical to predicting state support for research universities. After the results of the model are presented, three institutions and states are explored in-depth using a multi-case study design. The cases aim to bring to life the contextual factors not captured by the regression model. The following sections present the methods and findings for the multiple regression analysis.

RESEARCH QUESTION AND DEFINITION OF TERMS

Before the quantitative methodology is introduced, it is necessary to clearly define important terms in the research question. The research question, restated from chapter one, is as follows: What factors best explain the variation in state support for public research universities during the 1990s? Two key terms in this question merit clarification: state support and public research universities.

State Support

In this study, state support is defined as unrestricted state appropriations for public research I universities. This definition is made clear with the help of the annual finance survey conducted by the National Center for Education Statistics. The Center's Integrated Postsecondary Education Data System (IPEDS) survey solicits financial and other data from U.S. colleges and universities for the purpose of comparison and policy research. The survey defines unrestricted state appropriations as those state dollars received by the institution through acts of a legislative body, except for gifts and contracts. These state funds are provided to an institution with no limitations or stipulations placed on them by legislature. These funds are typically used for meeting current operating expenses, not for specific programs or projects. This definition excludes facilities budgets, special research programs, and exceptional units such as University Hospital and Clinics. On the other hand, this definition includes expenses such as faculty salaries, fringe benefits, maintenance costs, wages, equipment, fellowships, scholarships, and mandatory transfers (IPEDS, 1998).

Public Research Universities

Public research universities are defined using classification criteria established by the Carnegie Foundation for the Advancement of Teaching. Since 1970, the Carnegie Foundation has classified groups of U.S. colleges and universities according to their missions as a way to improve the precision of the Carnegie Foundation's research.

The Carnegie Foundation defines public research I universities as those state institutions that offer a full range of baccalaureate programs, are committed to graduate education through the doctorate, give high priority to research, award 50 or more doctoral degrees each year, and receive annually $40 million or more in federal support (carnegiefound.org, 1994). In the most recent edition, 1994, the Carnegie Foundation reported that fifty-nine institutions meet this criteria. Appendix A provides a list of all 59 institutions. The sample in this study investigates the entire population of institutions meeting the Carnegie definition of public research I university.

MULTIPLE REGRESSION ANALYSIS AND DATA COLLECTION

Data were collected from existing databases of all variables in the conceptual framework that were readily quantifiable and for which data were available. These data were analyzed using multiple regression to explore which factors identified in the conceptual framework best explain differences in unrestricted state appropriations for public research I universities.

Multiple regression is useful for this study because it allows researchers to examine separately the relationships between a series of independent variables and the dependent variable. The dependent variable in this study is unrestricted state appropriations for public research I universities. The independent variables are the multiple factors outlined in the conceptual framework that the literature cites as being useful to predict state appropriations for higher education. The variables in this framework can be reviewed in Figure 2:1, the fishbone diagram presented in chapter two. From this framework, twenty-six variables that were quantifiable and for which data were available were selected for analysis.

Table 3:1 outlines the description of each of the variables included in the regression analysis and how they fit into the study's conceptual framework. The data include economic and demographic variables such as per capita taxes and income, state population, state unemployment rate, population of "college age" residents (18-24 years old), the number of private and public universities in the state, and per capita expenditures on education, health care, and corrections. In addition, institutional characteristics were accounted for at each of the 59 public research I universities in the sample. These factors include total enrollment of full time undergraduate and graduate students, total tuition and fees revenue, total federal grants and contracts, and total campus expenditures on instruction, research, public service.

Several dichotomous variables were also included in the analysis, including the political party of the governor and majority of the legislature in office during budget creation. In addition, the governance structure was entered as a dichotomous variable, depending on whether the state operated a consolidated governing board structure, coordinating board (regulatory or advisory power), or planning and service agency. Appendix 2 provides the metric used for each variable.

The data used in the regression model were analyzed in one consolidated database covering two time periods, FY 1991-92 and FY 1996-97. FY 1991-92 was selected because it marked a critical downturn in state appropriations for higher education. For the first time in 33 years, the 1991-92 state budgets allotted less money to higher education than for the previous year (Schuh, 1993). Data from this period captured a budget year that was uniformly poor among colleges and universities. Fiscal year 1996-97 was selected because it was the most recent data available. A dummy variable was entered to account for differences between the two time periods.

Table 3:1 Conceptual Framework and Regression Model Variables

Economic and Demographic	Political Influences and Priorities	Type of Governance Structure	Institutional Characteristics
Total state population	Party majority (republican or democrat) lower house during budget creation	Consolidated governing board	Total enrollment: full time undergraduate students
Population of "college age" residents (18-24)	Party majority (republican or democrat) upper house during budget creation	Coordinating board: regulatory power	Total enrollment: full time graduate students
Per capita income	Republican or democratic governor during budget creation	Coordinating board: advisory power	Total tuition and fees revenue
Per capita taxes	Per capita spent on health care	Planning and service agency	Total private gifts and contracts
Employment rate	Per capita spent on corrections	Number of private 4-year institutions in the state	Total federal grants and contracts
	Per capita spent on education	Number of public 4-year institutions in the state	Expenditures on instruction
			Expenditures on research
			Expenditures on public service

The consolidated database focuses on aggregate state support for institutions as opposed to the change in support from FY 1991-92-1996-97. The purpose of the aggregate focus is to capture the most compelling factors that predict state support in periods of both low support (1991-92) and recovering support (1996-97). The goal of the analysis is to draw out the most stable factors which explain differences in state support over a longer term, regardless of short-term fluctuations in budgetary conditions. Combining the two databases provided a way to meet this objective. Appendix B provides a complete list of the data sources used to create the database and the metric used for each variable.

REGRESSION MODEL SELECTION

Three criteria were established to select the variables for inclusion in the final model. These criteria focus on the theoretical appropriateness, significance, and whether the model satisfies basic assumptions of normality and homogeneity.

Stated another way, three questions were answered affirmatively to create the best model for this analyses:

1) Does the model inform the theoretical framework in this study? Do the findings add to a conceptual understanding of the research question?

2) Does the data analysis suggest that the variables are significant or an important factor in predicting state support for research universities?

3) Does the model satisfy basic regression assumptions?

Driven by these criteria, I employed a three-phase method to generate findings to be used in forming conclusions. First, I conducted a significance test with the standard for variable exclusion set at .05. Simple regressions were run for each independent variable one the dependent variable—unrestricted state appropriations. Conducting this analysis helped me consider important variables to include in subsequent phases of the model building procedure.

Second, I included all combinations of variables in the model to see the effects of variable interaction on the significance levels among all variables. In other words, I reviewed whether the addition or subtraction of certain variables impacted the significance of other variables.

Third, I analyzed each model to determine whether they met basic regression assumptions of homogeneity and normality. The model that best fit these assumptions was selected as my final model.

FINDINGS AND CONCLUSIONS

While the results of any regression should be interpreted cautiously, the multi-step approach pointed to seven variables that best predict unrestricted state appropriations for research I universities. The model variables and scores are presented in table 3:2. Table 3:3 provides a description of the means, standard deviation, and correlation for the variables used in the regression.

This regression model provides some important clues to understanding variation in state support for research I universities. Specifically, it suggests that a state's tax rate, political climate, higher education governance structure, and institutional enrollment and expenditures are important factors determining the level of state support for these types of institutions. A few compelling findings offer some important contributions to the study's conceptual framework.

First, the model suggests that research I universities governed by a consolidated governing board are more likely to have higher appropriations than those governed by a coordinating board or planning and service agency. Specifically, the regression suggests that research institutions governed under this system, on average, receive $48.7 million dollars more in unrestricted state appropriations than institutions governed by other structures.

In addition, this model suggests that the political affiliation of the state legislature is also an important factor predicting support. In particular, research I universities are likely to have higher appropriations in states where Democrats control both the senate and assembly. The political composition of the assembly seems to especially make a difference. On average, research I universities receive an additional $26.6 million dollars a year in unrestricted appropriations when Democrats control the assembly as opposed to Republicans.

An important economic, and arguably political indicator, is the effect of the tax rate on state support. For every additional dollar in taxes collected per capita, one could forecast an additional $43.6 million dollars in unrestricted support for the research I university. Put simply, research I universities are likely to have higher appropriations in states with higher per capita taxes. This could be considered a logical indicator since higher taxes generally equate to more money spent on government programs.

Table 3:2 Regression Model: Factors for Predicting Unrestricted State Appropriations for Research I Universities

Variable	Unstandardized		Standardized	
	Beta	Std. Error	Beta	t-stat
Per capita taxes	43,687.125	12,143.110	.172	3.958*
Total state population	2.171	.662	.226	3.2778*
Democratic/Republican controlled State Senate	-26,656,832	9,560,708.70	-.148	-2.7888*
Democratic/Republican controlled State Assembly	-3,815,534	9,162,350.7	-.022	-.416
Research I University and all other state universities governed by a consolidated governing board	48,763,178	8,799,326.8	.253	5.542*
Number of public universities in the state	-783,341.9	477,112.67	-.109	-1.642
Total expenditures on public service	.663	.118	.271	5.620*
Total enrollment of full-time graduate students	10,040.236	2,819.615	.281	3.561*
Total expenditures on instruction	.416	.083	.428	4.983*

Finally, institutional characteristics were shown to be the most important predictors of unrestricted appropriations. The high standardized coefficients for instruction and public service indicate that expenditures are highly correlated and an important predictor. This correlation is also logical and expected since appropriations will likely reflect the budgetary needs for supporting the teaching and service missions of the institution.

Variable	Mean	SD	1	2	3	4	5	6	7	8	9
Per capita tax	1421.24	333.8	1.00								
Total population	9,955,980.5	9,019,758	.170	1.00							
Republican or Democrat majority in the State Senate	.41	.49	.217*	.025	1.00						
Republican or Democrat majority in the State Assembly	.34	.48	.011	-.180	.495**	1.00					
Consolidated Governing Board	.26	.44	-.038	-.281**	.069	-.017	1.00				
Number of 4-year Public Universities	17.65	12.08	-.009	.707**	-.054	.025	-3.64**	1.00			
Expenditures on Public Service	40,297,431	35,011,101	-.004	-.300**	.001	.022	.188*	-.327**	1.00		
Expenditures on Instruction	177,744,533	88,496,389	.319**	.302**	.189*	.117	-.060	.156	.243**	1.00	
Total enrollment of full-time graduate students	4,472.12	2,356.45	.075	.255**	.027	.118	-.021	.174	.186*	.816**	1.00
Dependent Variable: Unrestricted State Appropriations	1.9E +08	85,590,019	.325**	.228*	-.006	-.052	.226*	-.003	.442**	.780**	.719**

* Correlation is significant at the .05 level (2-tailed)
** Correlation is significant at the .01 level (2-tailed)

Table 3:3 Means, Standard Deviations, and Correlations for the Regression Variables

LIMITATIONS AND IMPLICATIONS FOR QUALITATIVE INVESTIGATION

The regression model has some limitations which are important to note. First, the two datapoints cover only a short five-year time period. Additional data covering a longer period would provide a more robust and comprehensive picture of reasons behind differences in state support for research universities. The consolidated database in this study provides only a snapshot of state support during one decade—the 1990s.

Furthermore, the small sample size may amplify the explanatory power of the variables. Since nine variables were used to explain 118 observations, it is not surprising that the final r^2 of the model was high at .821. At the same time, the adjusted r^2 accounts for the sample size and still produced a high adjusted r^2 of .806, suggesting the strength of the model's predictive power.

Another limitation is that there are many alternative definitions for the variables used in the regression, and I was forced to make choices about how to define various support indicators. Making choices such as these naturally affects the results of the regression model. For example, state tax capacity is one factor that could be measured in a number of ways. Layzell and Lyddon (1990) define state tax capacity as the amount of state revenue that would be generated if the revenue bases were tapped at the maximum allowable rates for taxes and service fees. The authors argue that the best measure of determining tax capacity is the underlying economic activity in a state, but that general sales volume, corporate income, personal income, and property values are other indicators to consider.

Finally, the model does not address the rich contextual differences that are likely to be present at each of the observed states and institutions. These differences would include the supporting theoretical strands not captured by the regression model such as state culture, historical support for the institution, and public attitudes toward the institution. Similarly, the effects of institutional strategies can not be considered in a strict application of the regression analysis. The fact is that relying on the regression model alone places limits on understanding the complete landscape of differences in state support for research universities.

In order to try to understand these differences, I sought to identify specific institutions that were not well predicted by the regression model—institutions receiving more or less appropriation than the model expects. I was able to conduct this analysis by plotting the regression residuals against fitted values. The residuals represent institutions within various standard deviations from the expected mean, given the effect of each factor in the model. Figure 3:1 illustrates how identifying outliers in the scatterplot can provide important implications for qualitative investigation. Reviewing the plot, one can see institutions that appear above or below the expected appropriations level based on model predictions. In other words, the model indicates a range of institutions that receive higher or lower state appropriations than predicted based on the nine variables in the model. Figure 3:1 illustrates the actual appropriation received by all public research I universities and the regression model predicts what each of these institutions should receive in appropriations. On the standardized residuals "X" axis, "0" represents the predicted appropriations line. 1 and 2 standard deviations above the line are those institutions that receive higher support than the model predicts, while −1 and −2 below receive lower support than predicted.

To explore unexplained factors in the model I sought to conduct a more in-depth analysis of three institutions falling under different levels of standard deviations: one falling 1 standard deviation below expected appropriations, one observation a standard deviation higher than predicted, and one well predicted by the model. The goal of this investigation was to isolate three institutions representing various support levels—low to high—based on model predictions.

Figure 3:1 highlights three institutions that meet these specifications. Specifically, the model suggested that Ohio State University (OSU) received less unrestricted appropriations than predicted based on the statistical analysis. The implication is that OSU received less state appropriations than its peers, based on this analysis. State appropriations for the University of Wisconsin-Madison (UW) were well predicted by the model, indicating that the variables were good indicators to predict unrestricted state appropriations for the UW. Finally, the model showed that the University of Georgia (UGA) received greater appropriations than predicted by the variables in the regression model. The implication is that UGA received more state support than its peers.

Figure 3:1 Case Study Selection Plot

Scatterplot
Dependent Variable: Unrestricted State Appropriations

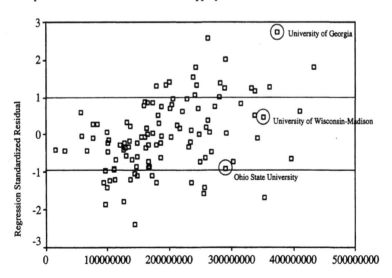

There is another important reason why these three institutions are highlighted over others in the scatterplot. These three institutions consistently appeared in each of their respective standard deviation levels, regardless of the variable or method of model building used to generate the graph. This observation is important because it suggests that there are other stable, less tangible factors present in these states and institutions that explain the reasons behind their placement on the graph. This important observation led me to a deeper investigation of the three institutions using qualitative methods.

QUALITATIVE METHODS

The regression model suggests that three institutions represent distinct variations in state appropriations for public research I universities: Ohio State University, (less than predicted appropriations) the University of Wisconsin-Madison, (predicted appropriations) and the University of Georgia (higher than predicted appropriations). In this phase of the study, qualitative methods are employed to provide a more in-depth look at each of these institutions and their host states. The goal of the qualitative analysis is to understand important contextual differences that exist between these entities which are difficult to capture using quantitative methods alone. Qualitative methods seek to provide richness and depth to understand the complexity of factors that play a role in state budgeting for higher education.

DATA COLLECTION AND THE POSITIONED SUBJECT APPROACH

Interviews and a document review were the primary methods of data collection employed in the multi-case study. To guide my interaction with the interviewees, I used a positioned subject approach as defined by Conrad, Howarth, and Millar (1993). The authors' define the positioned subject approach by identify several assumptions. To begin with, it is assumed that the researcher interprets and makes meaning of interview data based on his or her experiences and perspectives. Accordingly, it supposes that interviewees are people with particular needs, perceptions, and capabilities for action, and that an individual's position within the environment affects his or her responses. The totality of these factors influence the way subjects interpret and respond to the interview questions as well as the way that researchers' interpret and code responses (Conrad, Howarth, Millar, 1993).

A major premise in multi-case study design is that the sample must be representative of the population that it claims to represent (Conrad, Howarth, Millar, 1993). Stated another way, the study must enlist the perspectives of a diverse group of stakeholders that most affect and are affected by the particular phenomena. Using this reasoning, I identified the actors most integral to the higher education appropriations process as outlined in my conceptual framework.

Informed by my framework, I decided that campus administrators, board of regents staff, governance system executives, state relations staff, state legislators, department of administration staff, and the governor's office, were among the most important stakeholders to involve in my interviews. Furthermore, I acknowledged that informants among each stakeholder group must be evenly represented to reduce bias based on political ideologies or the shared perceptions of a given stakeholder group. Thus, I designated a small number of interviewees from each group to make up the entire sample representing each institution and state. The list and number of individuals interviewed by each stakeholder group are found in Table 3.4.

Table 3.4 Distribution of Interviewees by Stakeholder Group and Site

	State of Georgia, University of Georgia Campus	State of Wisconsin, University of Wisconsin-Madison Campus	State of Ohio, Ohio State University Campus
Campus state relations staff	1	1	1
Campus administrators	2	3	3
Governance System staff	2	1	1
State Department of Administration staff	3	2	2
State legislators (R)	2	3	1
State legislators (D)	2	3	2
Governor's Office staff	1	1	1
Total:	13	14	12

To identify the most informed individuals in each stakeholder group, I used the snowball sampling technique as explained by Bogdan and Bicklen (1992). Snowball sampling means that the first interviewee was asked to recommend others to be interviewed, and so on. The first person I interviewed was the state relations professional for each institution sampled. This individual was selected because I viewed them as most central to the activities involving state budgeting for the campus. I relied on this individual to provide names of others to interview from the other stakeholder groups. In turn, these individuals provided names of other informants in each stakeholder group to be approached for interviews.

Consistent with Conrad, Howarth, and Millar's positioned subject approach, I asked questions that were open ended, allowing interviewees to direct the discussion. I began interviews with the broad question, "Tell me about the factors that you believe best explain the level of state support for Institution X." Stating it a different way, I often outlined the question more informally: "From your perspective, what is happening in the State or on campus that best tell the story about state support for Institution X."

While this open-ended approach guided my interviews, I also created an interview protocol to assist my efforts. My protocol consisted of a broad set of topics and supporting questions that I derived from my conceptual framework.

My interview protocol can be found in Appendix C. All interviews were tape-recorded and transcribed with the permission of each subject.

Finally, I enriched my interviews by reviewing documents that were useful to inform my analysis. Most often these documents were referred by subjects during the interviews. The documents added detail to the concepts espoused by the interviewees and helped sig nificantly with my interpretation of the interview data. To analyze the data, I used the coding procedure as suggested by Bogdan and Bicklen (1992).

LIMITATIONS

The primary limitation of this multi-case study is the small number of institutions from which to draw conclusions about high, moderate, and low support conditions. As such, I can not completely rely on the three institutions to explain the entire universe of factors explaining differences in state support for research universities. In other words, an important limitation is that the findings from the qualitative study may not be fully generalizable across institutions and states.

A secondary limitation of this study is the modest number of interviews conducted in each state and institution. While data saturation was achieved among the sample, a more comprehensive list of interviewees would arguably have strengthened my findings and subsequent conclusions. Put simply, adding other voices would have provided greater wealth of perspectives. But due to time and financial limitations, I resolved to focus my efforts on key informants representing each major stakeholder group.

Finally, I recognize that some interviewees may have responded in ways that were politically savvy. Although I assured all subjects of complete confidentiality, it is possible that informants may have been inhibited to address areas that they perceived as politically sensitive. At the same time, I felt that most interviewees were genuine in their responses. In fact, most were eager to inform me on the topic from their point of view.

THREE CAMPUS INVESTIGATION

In the chapters that follow, the voices of interviewees tell a unique story about each of the states and institutions investigated in this study, focusing on the complex relationships between the campuses, states, and general citizenry in these regions. It through careful interpretation of these relationships that one can begin to understand the important differences in state support for the three institutions.

The case studies begin with an in-depth look at Ohio State University, followed by the University of Wisconsin-Madison, and finally the University of Georgia. The main themes that emerged from each case will be presented, discussed, and summarized in chapters four through six. In chapter seven, a cross-case analysis will be conducted to compare and contrast the main contextual differences revealed in the studies, and offer conclusions about factors most compelling to explain variations in support.

CHAPTER 4

Ohio State University

INTRODUCTION

When Ohio was granted statehood in 1803, it became home to a large group of European immigrants seeking fertile lands and an escape from the increasing population of the East Coast. These Ohio residents developed strong cities comprising a diverse assembly of Poles, Germans, Irish, Greeks, Hungarians and Slavs. For all the immigrants, agriculture was the predominant livelihood of the early to mid-1800s. Corn, wheat, and oats were the chief grains produced, whereas other farmers concentrated on raising hogs, sheep, and cattle. The strength of Ohio's agricultural economy is still evident today as Ohio ranks as a leader in the production of canned vegetables and meat products (Our Ohio, 1970).

Beyond agriculture, Ohio's valuable natural resources in Youngstown and the Mahoning Valley region helped the state transition into a strong industrial society during the late 19th century. Thanks to the strong presence of minerals, the state has become the major industrial power in the iron and steel industry for more than 100 years. In addition, Ohio continues to lead the nation in the manufacturing and export of rubber and plastics products. The state produces more than 1/3 of the tires and tubes manufactured in the United States and makes over 140 different products including bolts, metal products, office machinery, and soap (Our Ohio, 1970).

Founded in 1870, Ohio State University was established with the state's core agricultural and industrial strengths as a backdrop. The institution was formed as the state's land-grant university to "promote the education of the industrial classes." Out of this tradition, Ohio State University developed a broad curriculum to train Ohio residents in the area of agriculture and mechanics. Beyond these subjects, the early campus offered a wide range of courses in the liberal arts. Ohio State's breadth of educational opportunities still exists today as the institution offers 176 undergraduate majors and 220 graduate fields of study (OSU Website, 1999).

OSU owns the distinction as being among the largest state institutions in the country, enrolling 48,511 undergraduate and graduate students in 1998. Annual resident undergraduate tuition is currently $4,100, which places OSU among the most expensive institutions among its Big Ten peers. The breakdown of OSU's budget in Figure 4.1 reveals that the institution relies heavily on its extensive hospital revenue, supplementing modest support from state and federal sources. At 17.8 percent, OSU relies more heavily on student tuition and fees than UW and UGA (OSU Website, 1999). The revenue statistics for these campuses will be presented in a forthcoming section.

Finally, the expenditures pie chart shows that instruction, departmental research and the university hospital are dominant areas supported by OSU. Other units, such as public service, are allotted a very modest amount of money compared to other areas of the budget.

Ohio State University is one of 80 colleges and universities in the State of Ohio, of which 37 of these campuses are public institutions. The Ohio public universities are loosely governed under a coordinating board called the Ohio Board of Regents. The Board's primary responsibility is to plan for the overall needs of higher education in the state, and coordinate the efforts of campuses to fulfill these needs. The structure has little authority over the operations of the campuses.

As will be discussed in the next sections, the case study of Ohio and Ohio State University point to the importance of the state's economic history and political makeup in setting the precedent for the modest level of state support for OSU. Evidence suggests that the governance system has had an important impact, as well as the perception about OSU's commitment to fulfilling its role as the state's land grant university. From these general observations, four themes emerged to explain the modest to low level of state support for Ohio State University: history, higher education governance, political climate, and outreach and campus visibility.

HISTORY

As stated in the beginning of this chapter, the early settlers of Ohio created a strong industrial economy that has served the state well for many years. However, it is this history that seems to be detrimental to Ohio's investment in higher education. In particular, interviewees spoke about Ohio's prosperous manufacturing and industrial communities as a major hindrance toward support for higher education in the state. Explained one interviewee, "When economic times were good a lot of people in the state could make a good living by working in a steel mill, rubber factory, or machine shop… not by going to college. The success in industry created a general sentiment among the Ohio public that higher education was not necessary to advance oneself or society…..thus, higher education has always been an afterthought during budget creation." Added another, "The folks in the blue collar community view higher education as more of a luxury. It is a feeling that we're doing fine without it, so why spend money on it?" While most interviewees agreed that this sentiment is slowly changing, the theme still seems to run strong in some industrial circles in Ohio.

Source: Current Funds Budget 1996-97, Office of Resource Planning and Institutional Analysis, Ohio State University
http://www.rpia.ohio-state.edu/budget_planning/kbpd/cfb/cfb-1997.pdf

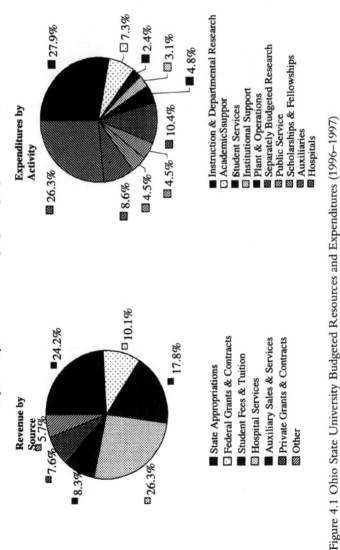

Figure 4.1 Ohio State University Budgeted Resources and Expenditures (1996–1997)

Data such as these suggest that the impact of higher education is not being felt outside of the individuals who benefit from earning a college degree in the state. Recognizing the disconnection between its blue-collar community and postsecondary education system in Ohio, OSU administrators face significant challenges in educating Ohio residents about the compelling purposes of higher education, which extend far beyond the classroom. The impact of higher education must be clearly articulated so that it can be shown to touch the lives of all citizens, including those in industrial communities.

Beyond its strong blue-collar culture, Ohio has long been a fiscally conservative state due to the low tax, low service philosophy of the Eastern European immigrants. The immigrants are credited with setting the precedent for the culture that still exists today. Interviewees explained that the forefathers' dominant political philosophy was that the burden of all costs must be placed on the user. Some pointed to this philosophy as explaining why Ohio is ranked 30th in state taxes and lower in service than other states.

Given this tradition, it makes sense then, why state appropriations are low and tuition is high for Ohio colleges and universities. Ohio citizens have long viewed higher education as more of a private good as opposed to a collective one. The underlying belief among the majority of the Ohio citizenry is that the student is the one benefiting from advanced education, so he or she should be the one to pay for it. Again, this rationale is credited with explaining why Ohio's tuition is currently the 9th highest in the country and why Ohio remains 41st among 50 states in per capita support for higher education.

Beyond the fiscally conservative culture, Ohio's recent economic history has also had an important affect on support for higher education. Like most states, the poor economy of the early 1990's hurt Ohio considerably. Higher education in Ohio was hit especially hard between 1990-1995. In fact, an OSU campus administrator confirmed that Ohio State University took the biggest budget cut among the "Big Ten" Universities during that period. But since the 1995 budget, state appropriations have improved with economic recovery. Appropriations have increased in an attempt to "make up" for the severe cuts earlier in the decade. Campus administrators report that the boost in support has returned appropriations levels near that of the late 1980s, a more stable, albeit still modest, time of funding for higher education in Ohio.

POLITICAL CLIMATE

Tied to Ohio's history and culture, the political climate in Ohio was an important theme that emerged regarding support for higher education in the state. The data suggests that gubernatorial and legislative priorities have played a very important role in determining the level of state support for Ohio State University. Equally important to this discussion are state agency officials' perceptions about the institution and its perceived responsiveness to the people of Ohio. The intersection of Ohio's culture and political agenda are clearly important to understanding the challenges that higher education institutions face in the state.

Gubernatorial Priorities and Perceptions

Former Governor George Voinovich was often cited as having an important role in determining OSU's fiscal fate during his eight-year term in office. Interviewees characterized the Governor's relationship with OSU as "rocky" and "dismal" when he took office in 1991. In short, study participants reported that the Governor felt that OSU was inefficient and spending too much and not living by his motto of "do more with less." In general, interviewees felt that the relationship was strained because of his perception that OSU was unresponsive about his expectations to make efficiency gains.

The Governor reportedly preached that the University needs to be more accountable and make selective investments. He also declared that the University needs to prioritize and set goals about where it most wants to excel. In 1992-93, OSU responded to the Governor's mandate to meet these goals. The institution restructured to be more efficient, more selective with admissions, and improve retention and quality of instruction.

For much of his term, Governor Voinovich perceived OSU to be unaccountable and inefficient which led to strained relationships between the governors office and OSU and subsequent declining interest in funding the institution. Because tax cuts were a major priority for the governor, he was most interested in OSU as it related to delivering an education that was efficient and funded by the user. Like other agencies in Ohio, higher education was to remain lean and efficient in its approach to delivering services. OSU struggled with meeting the governor's demands, which led to his criticism and reported ill will toward the university.

Added to these attitudes surrounding the institution, most interviewees agreed that higher education is simply not high on the Governor's priority list. Specifically, Voinovich was predominately interested in supporting the two-year college system because he viewed it as a more direct link to helping business and industry in the State. The Voinovich agenda points out the importance of linking higher education as a key mechanism to enhance economic growth. As the literature suggests, political leaders are drawn to the economic development appeal because it places higher education as a solution for sustaining the health of the state. Because the industrial communities in Ohio depend more on skilled labor in the factories and manufacturing plants, community colleges are in a better position to enhance their bargaining power than four-year institutions such as OSU.

Like many gubernatorial agendas across the country, Voinovich's priorities more clearly focused on K-12 schools, corrections, and Medicare. As "new federalism" has taken hold across the United States, governors are forced to commit additional resources to entitlement programs, leaving discretionary such as higher education as a secondary priority.

Legislative Priorities and Perceptions

Many legislative views about Ohio State University generally followed those of Governor Voinovich, concentrating concerns about OSU's lack of efficiency.

However, it is clear that the views are not completely one-sided. Of the legislators interviewed, a few gave high praise for the OSU's agricultural extension units that serve the rural areas. Some also recognized OSU's economic impact due to its expertise and leadership in technology and the supercomputer industry. These participants were more fully vested in the activities of particular OSU programs that served some compelling state interest.

But a more vocal group of legislators and state administrators had a completely different view of OSU—that OSU is arrogant and unconcerned about the needs of the State of Ohio. Said one interviewee, "They (OSU) only appear at the state house when they want money. The University is not there offering to help, they are just there begging. They are in the ivory tower doing research, but not helping down the street." Similarly there was criticism about OSU's approach to accountability. One legislator's perception is that OSU feels that they do not need to answer questions about how the money will be used. "Even with the emergence of performance-based funding emerging, this attitude prevails" noted one study participant.

Along the same lines, some legislators expressed the concern that OSU is too big. State officials note that parents complain that their kids are all being taught by teaching assistants and that there is not enough internal support for freshman entering the University. However, most interviewees holding the view felt that this is getting better, especially as OSU has placed more attention on retention issues in recent years.

Like Governor Voinovich, Ohio legislators are more focused on a number of priorities that compete with higher education. In particular, K-12 schools have demanded a great deal of attention due to a Supreme Court case ruling that Ohio's K-12 financing plan is unconstitutional. In short, the Court ruled that Ohio's plan relies too much on local property taxes to finance the schools. The effect is that the State has to make up for this inequality by spending more money on capital needs. Thus, more tax revenues are being diverted to meet these court mandates, meaning less money for other discretionary programs such as higher education.

Corrections was also identified as an area that is continuing to take a bigger slice of the Ohio budget. Most interviewees were careful to point out that corrections is not a priority, but that the social condition of the State forces lawmakers to spend money on it. Overall, interviewees suggested that the top legislative priorities are K-12 schools, corrections, Medicaid/human services, and higher education. Like Governor Voinovich, it was emphasized that some legislators greatly favor two-year schools over four-year colleges. The magnitude of the two-year schools was pointed out by one interviewee, "In Ohio, there are fifty two-year schools in the state, which means that almost every legislator has a technical school in their district. Of course, these schools will remain an important focus."

This statement provides useful insight into the critical role of Ohio technical colleges. Because technical colleges supply businesses with skilled labor, they are viewed as most intimately tied to advancing the economic goals of the state. As later sections of this chapter will discuss, OSU administrators are attempting to make a case for stronger investment in four year colleges as being critical to the economy of the 21st Century. This will be necessary in order to strengthen its partnership with the State of Ohio.

HIGHER EDUCATION GOVERNANCE

Higher education governance and the strength of regional campuses in Ohio are also important factors explaining the modest to low level of state support for Ohio State University. Interviewees explained that Ohio is more of a collection of large cities, or "city states" as one described the metro areas of Toledo, Cleveland, and Cincinnati. Citizens in these "city states" reportedly have strong commitments to their regional or metro universities. Cleveland State, Kent State, and the University of Cincinnati are just a few examples of institutions that have gained the loyal support of their regional residents. Because of the strength of these local universities, Ohio State University is not warmly viewed as Ohio's flagship campus. In fact, one interviewee declared that referring to OSU as the flagship institution would be "fighting words" in some areas. This may be an important observation addressing OSU's funding struggles, because it suggests that the strength of the institution's identity varies considerably across the state. In Ohio, "turf issues" are clearly a barrier to OSUs efforts in claiming leadership on many fronts in Ohio's postecondary education system. Because legislators represent the interests of their regions, they are less inclined to support an institution that might be viewed as competing or duplicating the work of universities in their districts. The territorial nature of Ohio's higher education system adds to the cultural challenges that OSU faces in its attempt to partner more firmly with the state.

Adding to these struggles over turf, the governance structure itself is seen to be a detriment to all Ohio universities, including OSU. Ohio operates a coordinating board called the Ohio Board of Regents. Like most coordinating boards, the Board does not set policy for the institutions, but rather assists with planning for the overall higher education needs in Ohio. The vast majority of interviewees reported that the coordinating board system is an ineffective way to manage Ohio's public colleges and universities. Most interviewees claimed that the Board's authority is weak, which has resulted in a lack of coordination between institutions. Specifically, the weakness has allowed duplicative and competitive programs and missions to exist throughout higher education institutions in the State.

OSU interviewees declared that the coordinating board factor has been especially detrimental to Ohio State. Said one campus interviewee, "Not having a system hurts Ohio State because too many institutions are trying to offer the same programs that we are. There is jealousy among campuses, and for the most part, legislators are only concerned about the University in their backyard. For a long time there has been no real plan to keep institutions in check...this sucks up money from OSU." Other state officials told the same story, "For a long time the coordinating board did little and was ignored. If a campus wanted something it would run to the legislature. Right now there is still duplication and big holes, but this is beginning to change."

Most interviewees reported positive change because recent initiatives led by the Ohio Board of Regents helped to improve the coordination of some higher education programs across the State. Specifically, the Governor appointed *Higher Education Funding Commission* has restored some unity among campuses because it is pushing to tie state appropriations to institutional missions. In short, the Board has taken a more comprehensive look at the needs of the State and how the particular campuses can fulfill these needs. In one example, the Regent's Managing for the Future Taskforce has reviewed of all programs in the state and made recommendations about trimming duplicative Ph.D. programs. In addition, accountability efforts have increased since March 1997, as campuses were required to start submitting quarterly reports on accountability.

Finally, the Ohio Board of Regents is phasing out its current enrollment-driven formula to a more performance-based one. OSU interviewees applaud the measure because enrollment cutbacks planned at institution would mean that OSU would take cuts in appropriations. Having performance funding will provide an opportunity to show accountability in areas of research, access, and economic development in a way that will not negatively affect appropriations.

In sum, OSU faces formidable challenges with funding due to a number of cultural and structural issues surrounding its higher education governance structure. The territorial nature of the state has been exacerbated by the operation of a weak form of system governance. Although meaningful reform has been made in the area of performance-based funding, OSU will continue an uphill battle with separating itself as a distinct institution that merits special budgetary consideration. These challenges contribute greatly to OSU's struggles in obtaining higher levels of state support .

CAMPUS VISIBILITY AND OUTREACH

Because of Ohio's strong "city-state" culture and the extent of institutional competition in the state, OSU struggles significantly with its visibility across the Ohio. In fact, the lack of visibility of the OSU campus has been an important factor contributing to the funding struggles that OSU has faced in the past decade. Interviewees explained that OSU leadership has historically maintained a low profile in its involvement with the State and City of Columbus. On the positive side, former OSU President, Gordon Gee raised the visibility of the campus because of his extensive travel throughout various communities in Ohio. Interviewees agree that Gee took an active role in bringing the campus to the State, considerably more than most OSU presidents.

In addition, the agricultural school was cited as being visible and widely recognized as fulfilling the outreach component of the university land-grant mission. However, most reported that this did not hold true for other parts of campus. One OSU interviewee even made the leap that increased visibility of OSU programs would have a positive effect on state appropriations. Summed up the participant, "Agriculture outreach has been very successful. If all the departments were as successful with outreach as agriculture, we (OSU) wouldn't have a problem with funding." As an interviewer, I got the general sense that this statement spoke a lot to the current plight of OSU and its lack of success in garnering state support. I found it interesting that a number of interviewees, from both the state and campus side, implied the correlation between funding support and service to the state.

This link is becoming especially obvious to a growing number of OSU administrators who are trying to promote OSU as the state's economic engine. Many administrators have argued that OSU has long been an economic generator but that the campus simply does not get credit for it. While former President Gordon Gee helped to communicate the importance of research and technology, technology transfer, and partnerships, the interviewees reported that this effort was largely one-dimensional. One state official suggested that the economic development message is not taken to heart because OSU is approaching the subject in the wrong way. Said the interviewee, "They (OSU) are looking at economic impact by the dollars that come in, the number of new jobs, etc... Instead, they should be thinking of it as an investment in services to raise Ohio's quality of life. It's more than just jobs and money... they should focus on developing good K-12 schools. High quality schools bring in industry because CEO's won't feel they have to sacrifice their child's education to come to Ohio."

Beyond these struggles to establish itself as the state's economic engine, competition between Ohio institutions seems to impede OSU's visibility as the state's land grant university. Outreach at Kent State University, legislative training sessions at Cleveland State, and economic development at the University of Akron were cited as successful outreach programs independent of OSU. Interviewees report that the outreach efforts between Ohio institutions are not well coordinated or understood among campuses. The competition and lack of coordination is detrimental to the OSU campus because legislators are only exposed to the outreach work of institutions in their own districts. Thus, Ohio State's role as the state land-grant institution is seemingly minimized due to other campus initiatives.

In sum, lack of visibility is an important factor contributing to the struggles that OSU faces in its attempt to forge stronger alliances with the state. Many interviewees commented on OSU's presence due to its strong football program, but pointed to the uphill battle that OSU faces as it markets itself as a strong state resource. The strategies for communicating the accomplishments and merits of the institution are continually reevaluated as administrators seek to paint a positive picture of OSU to state officials and the public at large.

Communication Strategy and Structure

OSU administrators told me a great deal about the structures and strategies they have employed in an attempt to improve OSU's image. One campus administrator summed up their challenge, "We need to help the public and legislature understand that innovation comes out of the University. We're trying to improve the way we get this message out... targeting specific messages to legislators about what the campus is doing with cancer research, technology transfer, the research park, and business incubator. Another challenge is to make it clear that well qualified PhDs can bring in more business to Ohio."

Like many campuses, OSU is targeting its messages to appeal to the larger state needs of economic development. The strategy refocuses the message on the merits of its collective good rather than the private good. In other words, the strategy seeks to change the cultural perception that the individuals who benefit from earning college degrees are the primary beneficiaries of higher education. Instead, the focus on the societal benefits of state investment in higher education is meant to engage a wider audience of lawmakers and citizens in discussions about expanded funding opportunities. Currently there are plans to assemble an Ohio Business Council as a way to carry this message and gain political support for OSU as an economic engine. OSU administrators are still in the planning stages of this organization that will act as an outside advocate for higher education in Ohio.

A problem that contributes to Ohio State University communication problems is its outreach and public affairs structure. OSU operates no formal university relations structure to focus the outreach and economic impact messages across OSU schools and colleges. Instead, an informal body called the *Outreach and Engagement Council* has been formed as a way to coordinate the university relations efforts on the campus. At present, all outreach at OSU is coordinated at the school and college level. One interviewee commented that the decentralized approach, size of the campus, and diversity of messages being sent out from the various units makes it difficult to focus on developing an institutional message in support of the campus. This lack of coordination was evident in my interviews, as administrators representing different areas of the campus were often unclear themselves about the outreach activities in the institution.

Because of this informal approach to communication and outreach, legislators and the public are likely to have difficulty navigating the campus to tap into its essential resources. In this regard, important opportunities to showcase the campus are lost due to the sheer size and breadth of campus units and programs. Restoring the faith of state officials and the public depends on OSU's ability to successfully engage these constituents in the vital programs of the campus. The outcomes of these programs, and how they benefit the state, must be apparent to those who are supporting them.

Faculty Rewards for Public Service

Designing strategies for communicating to state officials and the public is only one small piece toward effectively demonstrating OSU's value to the state. Most important, the institution must convincingly model its commitment to serving the state through its faculty, students, and programs. OSU has struggled with maintaining its image as the land-grant institution because of legislative and public views about OSU's commitment to its public service mission.

A general perception exists among Ohio legislators and state administrators that OSU does little to encourage or reward the public service component in the faculty job description. During more than one interview with state administrators, a particular story was advanced as evidence of OSU's lack of commitment to public service. In short, it was reported that an assistant professor worked diligently on K-12 finance problems in Ohio as a piece of his public service duties. State officials said that the work of the professor was unprecedented and as one state interviewee put it, "made a better contribution to the State of Ohio than any OSU professor in the history of the institution." Soon after his well-publicized contribution, interviewees reported that the professor was denied tenure because he failed to adequately publish in scholarly journals. State officials were outraged by this action. Said one interviewee, "This incident clearly sent the message to the State that public service is not valued by OSU. We hear the message of public service in speeches but don't see it in practice." Many interviewees reported that this well publicized failure undercut former President Gordon Gee's effort to show the value of OSU to the State. Declared one state official, "The President (Gee) can talk all he wants, but it's just not happening."

Stories such as this are deeply damaging to institutions such as OSU because they are often held up to represent the entire institution. Such stories become symbols by which lawmakers and the public understand higher education to be mired in the "publish or perish" standard in today's research universities. Effective partnerships with states and research institutions rely on institutional commitments to serving states that are deeply reflected in mission and practice.

SUMMARY

After reviewing this case study it is easy understand why the battle for state funds for Ohio State University has been largely uphill. In fact, one could argue that the institution began "in the hole," as Ohio's blue-collar heritage immediately set the stage for modest investment in higher education. Today, Ohio's historical backdrop can be credited with the present political orientation of Ohio's elected officials and their philosophy that the burden of higher education expenses is not the state's responsibility.

But Ohio State faces other formidable challenges. First, the weak coordinating board structure in Ohio seems to preclude the equitable and efficient use of the state's already modest allocation of resources. The competition between institutions is clearly a detriment to funding opportunities for OSU, mostly because Ohio legislators and the public at-large seem to only care about institutions in their own district. Thus, when the weakness of the coordinating board is combined with the loyalty and strength of Ohio's "city states," it is sure to result in financial struggles for the state's pseudo-"flagship" institution.

Finally, it is an understatement to say that Ohio State's attempts to market outreach and public service are failing. This became clear to me when some interviewees even argued against the very existence of outreach at OSU. Rather, this study suggests that OSU's outreach component is largely one-dimensional (agricultural focus) and that the institution's message about public service is simply viewed as an unfulfilled promise. Beyond the rhetoric, the institution appears to be hurt by its decentralized approach in its outreach efforts. Because of the size and complexity of the institution, successful public service efforts are apt to be lost in the noise. Simply put, the informal structure of the outreach component adds to Ohio State's marketing problems. Surrounding all of these issues is the question of OSU's commitment to the public service mission of the institution. While communication strategy and university relations structure is important, it is empty without real commitment to serving the needs of the state. An honest evaluation of OSU's practices related to service and outreach is critical to begin strengthening its partnership with the State of Ohio.

CHAPTER 5

University of Wisconsin-Madison

INTRODUCTION

A host of images have come to define Wisconsin's unique character over its 150-year history. Long known as "America's Dairyland," Wisconsin is most famous for the quality of its cheeses and quantity of its milk production. Some also point to Wisconsin's many natural assets that have put the state in the forefront of major manufacturing industries. Papermaking, brewing, and meat processing have been important drivers for the state's economy in past decades.

But beyond cheese and beer, Wisconsin enjoys a reputation as having a dynamic and rich political history. The state's distinction as a progressive national leader emerged through the movement led by Robert M. La Follette in the early 20th century. The former governor and U.S. Senator pioneered far-reaching government reforms including the civil service system, consumer protection, and worker 's compensation (Keane and Ritsche, 1998).

Among LaFollette's many important contributions was his commitment to make higher education accessible to the common people of the state. Through the vision of LaFollette and early 20th century UW President Charles Van Hise, the nationally recognized Wisconsin Idea was born—the concept that the boundaries of the university are the boundaries of the State. Translated into action, the Wisconsin Idea most clearly benefited rural Wisconsin as UW faculty transferred agricultural breakthroughs directly to the farmers' fields. In the early part of the century, public policy was also commonly created with the help of UW faculty experts (Keane and Ritsche, 1998). It was during this period that an important precedent was set—that the University of Wisconsin-Madison was to be an active partner in solving state problems and shaping Wisconsin's economic future.

Established in 1848, the UW-Madison was among the first acts passed by the Wisconsin legislature. Signed into law by Wisconsin's first governor, Nelson Dewey, the first UW degrees were awarded in 1854 (UW-Madison Website, 1999). As the state's land-grant university, UW-Madison has a multifaceted mission, encompassing the roles of instruction, research, and public service. Of the three roles, research has arguably gained the university the most national attention. Today, the University of Wisconsin-Madison stands among the list of the most distinguished universities in the United States. Its graduate degree programs have gained national acclaim, as UW graduate degrees have been ranked in the top ten of every major academic publication since 1910 (UW-Madison Website, 1999).

While the quality of the UW is high, the tuition remains low. Undergraduate resident tuition at UW-Madison is currently $3,470 per year, among the lowest of its peer institutions in the Big Ten. UW-Madison's sources of revenues greatly reflect its national stature, as the campuses overall budget is boosted tremendously by federal dollars. Figure 5.1 provides a breakdown of UW-Madison's budget by source, showing that the primary funding sources are divided fairly evenly among state and federal sources, with the balance being picked up by grants and contracts, tuition, and sales. This observation speaks to the national focus of UW-Madison, as federal dollars play a very significant role in the life of the institution.

Finally, the pie chart illustrating expenditures by activity further demonstrates UW-Madison's focus as a national research center. Over 31 percent of the UW budget is earmarked for research compared to a smaller 22.9 percent for instruction, and 6.4 percent for public service.

Like Ohio State University, UW-Madison also serves a large student population. Total enrollment of undergraduate and graduate students in 1998 reached 40,109. UW-Madison is one of thirteen campuses managed by the University of Wisconsin System. The UW System is overseen by the Board of Regents—a consolidated governing board created through a merger of the Wisconsin State Universities and UW-Madison in 1971.

The case study of the State of Wisconsin and UW-Madison point to the importance of Wisconsin's present political context juxtaposed to its historical commitment to ensuring quality, access, and affordable higher education. As the following sections address, the universities changing role in relation to the Wisconsin Idea tells an important story about the campuses ability to garner state support in recent years. These concepts are organized into four main themes that collectively explain the moderate or predicted level of state support for UW-Madison: historical support, political climate, higher education governance, and campus visibility and outreach.

HISTORY

Because of the precedent set by Wisconsin's progressive movement, the UW-Madison and the other UW campuses have historically been well supported by the state. Wisconsinites of the past and present continue to place a high value on higher education with respect to quality, access, and affordability. For most of this century, higher education policy decisions have been with these core values as a backdrop.

However, during the mid-1980s a public sentiment developed that overall taxing and spending in Wisconsin should be closer to the national average. The beginning of a conservative trend started in response to the widely publicized fact that Wisconsin was among the highest taxed states in the nation. In December of

Source: 1998-99 Data Digest (trend data). Office of Budget, Planning & Analysis, University of Wisconsin-Madison http://www.bpa.wisc.edu

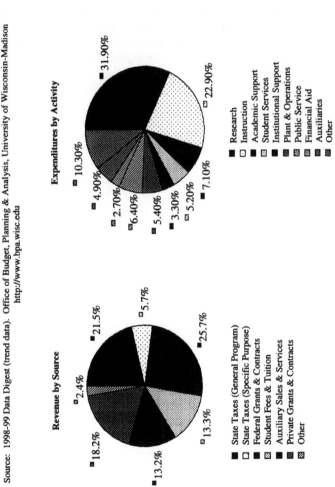

Figure 5.1 University of Wisconsin-Madison Budgeted Resources and Expenditures (1996–97)

1986, the Wisconsin Expenditure Commission acknowledged the state's high taxation, and reported that spending should be controlled and reduced. The Commission's recommendations document declared that "by any objective measure, Wisconsin is a high spending state" and that "the state develop long term spending targets that take into consideration the consideration of costs and benefits." The report showed that support for the UW System was particularly high during the early-mid 1980s. During the FY 1983-84, for example, Wisconsin ranked 3rd in the nation in the percentage of its residents enrolled in higher education, and 5th in per capita expenditures on higher education. In addition, Wisconsin's total spending for postsecondary education as a percentage of personal income ranked 10th and was 52 percent above the national average.

Of the many recommended cutbacks, the Commission targeted reduced spending on the UW system. Among other suggestions, the Commission called for limits on the number of students enrolled in the system, an adjustment in tuition levels so that a higher proportion of instructional costs would be paid by the users, and for private higher education to be better utilized as a way of bringing about savings to the UW System. The result of the Commission's work included an enrollment management policy to bring down costs for the UW System. The goal was to ensure that the quality of higher education would remain high in Wisconsin, but that fewer residents would be served. Most interviewees agreed that Governor Tommy Thompson was elected, in part, on the low-tax message of the expenditure commission's recommendations.

Like the State of Ohio, Wisconsin's history has played an important role in determining present-day levels of state support for UW-Madison. As a high tax state, Wisconsin also provides high services which includes higher education. From its inception, the state made a commitment to higher education as a key ingredient for developing the state's economy. Through inventions of UW diary scientist such as Harry Steenbock and Stephen Babcok, the state realized its full potential in its agrarian economy during the early years of the 20th Century.

But due to the success of UW's past service to the state and the generous investment of state dollars in the institution, the expectations for strong state support and strong service to the state are high on both ends of State Street. In other words, the state expects that the UW will continue its leadership in outreach in the spirit of the Wisconsin Idea. Meanwhile, UW administrators expect the state to continue its historic commitment to provide strong state funding for the institution.

But the culture of Wisconsin has clearly changed as the conservative policies of the last decade made its way onto the UW campus. Accountability for the UW was emphasized more fully and addressed real issues about how the UW impacts the day-to-day lives of Wisconsin residents. At the same time, state priorities have shifted to focus on entitlement programs and the effort to reduce taxes. The University and state are in a period of transition of understanding how they might best work together for the mutual benefit of the state. The future partnership between the state and UW-Madison lie in important conversations about the 21st Century and how they will integrate to create a stronger future for

Wisconsin residents. In Wisconsin, the governor has a pivotal role in advancing these conversations.

POLITICAL CLIMATE

Gubernatorial Priorities and Perceptions

During the past sixteen years, Governor Thompson's priorities have had a tremendous impact on the level of state support for higher education in Wisconsin. Higher education clearly stands behind the Governor's priorities of K-12 refinancing, property tax relief, and corrections. In particular, interviewees cited the Governor's commitment to cover two-thirds of the cost of K-12 schools as a major detriment to expanded funding opportunities for the UW. Among education initiatives, Governor Thompson is especially supportive of school-to-work and technology in the classroom. Adequately training people for jobs is a high priority for the Governor.

Throughout his administration, corrections has been a major piece of the Governor's agenda. In a five-year period, the corrections budget has grown by 105 percent, accounting for 4.6 percent of the budget in 1997. Interviewees reported that corrections and the K-12/property tax relief initiative has had a phenomenal impact on the budget, and consequent spending on higher education. As one interviewee put it, "After two-thirds of K-12 costs and corrections are covered there's just not much left in the pot to spend on higher education. The Governor simply has a different agenda."

Most interviewees agreed that the Governor is most receptive to exciting higher education initiatives such as BadgerNet (the state computer network), and the biotechnology center. One interviewee said, "The Governor likes high-profile programs, but not bread and butter resources like libraries, books and journals." Beyond these initiatives, the majority of campus interviewees suggested that the Governor has negative feelings for the UW-Madison for two reasons. First, the Governor believes that UW-Madison programs do not necessarily benefit the average resident. Or as one interviewee put it, "UW-Madison's agenda does nothing to help the people in Elroy." Second, most campus administrators explained that the relationship between the Governor and UW Chancellors have been strained since the days of former Chancellor Donna Shalala. Because of their politically polar viewpoints, the Governor and Shalala disagreed on a number of issues.

It is clear that important parallels exist between the gubernatorial agendas and attitudes toward the major research universities in Ohio and Wisconsin. Both republican governors have concentrated on issues of efficiency and accountability in their states. In Wisconsin, a call for lower taxes increased pressure on the governor to evaluate spending on state agencies, including its colleges and universities. Ohio is similar in that Governor Voinovich emphasized efficiency and accountability throughout state agencies. In both administrations, the governors have focused more squarely on entitlement programs such as K-12 education, healthcare, and corrections programs. Because of the significant resources that these programs demand, little room is left for the expansion of higher education budgets.

Although the issue of competing priorities is a major piece of the concern for research universities in Ohio and Wisconsin, it is just as important to note the similar attitudes of governors in these states. Both Voinovich and Thompson have expressed their concern that OSU and UW are out of touch with their communities. The prevailing theme that draws the governors to the institution is the prospect of expanded economic development opportunities for their states. Looking at both Ohio and Wisconsin, it is clear that investment in OSU and UW is contingent on the extent to which these institutions can fulfill these objectives for their states.

Legislative Priorities and Perceptions

Like Ohio, Wisconsin's legislative agenda closely reflects the gubernatorial agenda and consequently state support for the UW-Madison. Thus, the main priorities of the legislature include K-12 refinancing for property tax relief, corrections, and cutting taxes.

First, the legislature stands behind the Governor's commitment to fund two-thirds of the cost of K-12 schools because of its promise to reduce the burden of property taxes. Second, the corrections budget is increasing in response to handling the crime problem in the state. Most interviewees expressed frustration over this issue yet didn't offer alternatives to it. As one legislator put it, "We feel we have no choice but to deal with this [issue of incarcerating criminals]. The same holds true for health care and our aging population. We are forced to commit the resources."

Because Wisconsin still remains among the highest taxed states, legislators are continually pressured to cut taxes. The political rhetoric prevails, especially during election time, that Wisconsin should strive to bring the tax rate closer to national average. When it comes to prioritizing funding for higher education one legislator seemed to speak for everyone, "The UW stands on top of the nice to do list. The fact is that full attention can't be given because of other obligations and statuary commitments. The state will continue to provide steady support, as long as the System monitors its accountability."

Recognizing legislative perceptions about UW-Madison is also an important piece to consider when understanding where the institution sits in regard to state support. Perceptions of UW-Madison among legislators vary considerably. Of the legislators I interviewed, most felt that UW-Madison provides an important benefit to the state in the form of well-qualified graduates. Along the same lines, most legislators agree that that the academic quality of the UW is high and that parents in their districts are proud to send their kids to UW-Madison.

At the same time there is contingent of legislators, republican and democratic, that hold strongly negative views of UW-Madison. Legislators used the words "ungrateful, out-of-touch, and unable to demonstrate their worth" to describe the activities of the university. A main theme among the more hostile group of legislators was that the university remains an "ivory tower" and is elitist in attitude. One legislator felt that the university needed to be put in its place, commenting, "like it or not they are a state agency just like everybody else." In addition, legislators seemed to corroborate around the point that UW-Madison doesn't appreciate what the legislature does for it. One interviewee spoke for many, "The UW is never satisfied, and we never hear a thank you. We are at the point that we can never do enough, so why bother trying?"

Added to these tensions, some legislators commented about more obvious and measurable accountability problems. One legislator explained how the university did not appropriately deploy state dollars to help meet instruction needs. This allegedly caused mistrust among legislators in the early 1990s. In addition, a few legislators pointed to studies showing that faculty members only teach four hours a week.

While the aforementioned criticisms of UW-Madison prevail, most interviewees concurred there is an enormous public affection for the institution. Although broad base of public support exists for the university, interviewees agree that there is not a true understanding or appreciation for what the university is doing for the State. Said one campus voice, "We have to have passion... we need to humanize the university and become more effective in speaking the language of the average resident. The UW has not done a good job of selling itself." Added another campus interviewee, "The University needs to educate the legislators; they don't see successes and our impact on the state's economy."

This point became particularly clear during interviews with state officials. State officials admitted that they are largely unaware of the economic impact of the UW. Said one interviewee, "The impact of the university is largely unknown. How often have they (the UW) helped state agencies?" Some suggested that the UW System, in general, doesn't advertise itself well. One offered her advice, "I don't think the System as a whole tells us much. We get one report every year or something... but it doesn't get recognized. What you need is to string this out over a 12-month period, and make sure that you have success stories all the time. Talk about the economic impact it (the UW) has on the State and some success stories of what the kids think of the education they received. Advertise yourself. We don't know what you're doing." In the view of legislators, the impact is measured primarily in the number of quality students that graduate and enter the Wisconsin workforce. Other benefits to the state are less obvious and not communicated effectively to the legislature.

Finally, outside factors like the current enrollment management plan has negatively affected public attitudes toward UW-Madison. The scaled back enrollment over the past five years has resulted in fewer acceptances to the University, meaning that rising academic standards has precluded admission for even strong Wisconsin high school students. Parents of rejected student applicants are becoming increasingly disgruntled asking why their taxpayer dollars should go to pay for an institution that is not accessible to their own kids.

This discussion leads to further questions about the taxpayer's responsibility in financing a UW education. While Wisconsin has historically maintained a low tuition policy in keeping with the core values of access and affordability, there is a growing sentiment that tuition should be raised to accommodate for portions of funding that the state no longer supports. Added to this rationale for raising tuition, many feel that the quality of the UW-Madison necessitates an increased sharing of costs among students. Because the quality of the institution is so high, degree recipients should be expected to pay for this added quality, say some state officials. However, this view is still divided heavily among legislators, with a vocal contingent even arguing for tuition freeze. Advocates of the tuition freeze argue that affordability is a long-standing value that the state should proudly continue. "Why should we compromise offering an affordable education to our state residents?" said one interviewee. "We should be proud that we can provide high quality AND affordable education." During my interviews it became clear that the tuition issue will be increasingly important in future budget debates.

CAMPUS VISIBILITY AND OUTREACH

The Wisconsin Idea

Surrounding legislators' views about UW-Madison was their general perception about the institution's decreased commitment to outreach and public service. Many interviewees discussed UW-Madison's visibility and commitment to outreach in the context of the famed Wisconsin Idea. As I pointed out in the introduction of this chapter, the Wisconsin Idea has defined much of the state's relationship with the university over the past ninety years. During my interviews it quickly became clear that the Wisconsin Idea is best known by its past glory, not its present commitment. Most often, interviewees gave examples of how outreach of the early century was evident and direct in its benefits to the common citizen. "Grandpa used to have a high regard for UW even though he was never a student" said one interviewee. "UW faculty significantly helped him in the fields which made an impact on his life and livelihood." Another participant remarked, "It used to be that all the legislators downtown knew the UW faculty. Now nobody really knows any of the faculty members. UW used to play a serious role in helping shape state policy, but that is no longer the case." One study participant best summed up most interviewees' perceptions about UW-Madison's commitment to the Wisconsin Idea, "People are happy and proud of the University and its quality, especially when the football team or basketball team does really well. But the UW is living on a reputation from the past. When you ask, 'What does the Wisconsin Idea mean to you today,' it's hard for them to give you an explanation."

The source of these sentiments seemingly reflect a growing concern that the UW has become increasing national and international—no longer grounded in its rural roots. For example, one interviewee commented that the UW business school is being promoted as national and corporate center as opposed to a place to benefit state commerce. This statement seems to be representative of a larger perception that the UW is backing out of helping the "real" people of Wisconsin. Among interviewees there is a real sense that the university is straddling its interests of maintaining its local commitments and furthering its national reputation. Naturally, this fuels the argument that the state owes less to the university since it is shifting its focus to be more national. In response to this pressure, campus administrators have put a new spin on the Wisconsin Idea declaring that "the boundaries of the university are now the boundaries of the world." Despite this argument, most agree that the Wisconsin Idea needs to be updated for the 21st century to include the interests of Wisconsin's average resident.

Again, the parallels that exist between the external perceptions of UW and OSU are worth noting. An overriding attitude prevails that the two campuses are unresponsive to the needs of their states and are not serious about their public service missions. At the center is distrust among legislators about the motives of the institutions, and how closely tied they are to the states that support them. As the public missions of UW and OSU drifts, so does the state support for these institutions.

Campus Structures, Communication, and Strategy

Through my interviews I identified an important link between the structure of the outreach and communication function and the success of getting the word out about UW-Madison's contributions to the State. Like OSU, each UW school and college outreach initiatives are largely decentralized, operating their own outreach activities largely independent of other campus units. In the same way, no formal university relations structure exists at UW-Madison to focus or coordinate the outreach and public service messages across the institution. Similar to OSU's *Outreach and Engagement Council*, UW-Madison's *University Relations Team* was formed to coordinate the university relations efforts on the campus.

UW interviewees corroborated with OSU administrators remarks that the decentralized approach, size of the campus, and diversity of messages being sent makes it difficult to focus on an institutional message. Put simply, the present structure of the outreach and university relations function precludes the institution's ability to develop a successful communication plan—one that is coordinated and integrated to reflect the multiple contributions of the campus. The UW and OSU cases suggest that a cohesive framework for communicating with the public is necessary for research universities to help their diverse constituencies properly navigate the institution.

As it stands, the Office of the Chancellor at UW-Madison has developed its own state relations strategic plan is to publicize the campuses impact on the people in Wisconsin. Specifically, the plan calls for improved publications and building stronger relationships with legislators, state citizens, and alumni through the Office of the Chancellor. In conjunction with the Wisconsin Alumni Association's Badger Action Network (BAN), the Office has built a political coalition of UW alumni who seek to promote grass roots support for

UW-Madison. In addition, the university relations efforts focus on promoting campus visits by legislators, and recognizing UW advocates in the legislature.

While these activities are important, they fail to address a comprehensive plan to infuse UW-Madison back into the communities they historically served in the early part of the century. A strong partnership between the UW and state in the future is contingent on the institution's ability to reclaim its relevance to the people of Wisconsin. Simply put, state relations plans are empty without real action to deepen activities that will reconnect the institution to Wisconsin residents. The financial erosion that has faced the institution during the last decade is a reflection of the UW's failure to demonstrate its commitment to the state. This important issue will have to be addressed before the institution can make strides towards reclaiming stronger state support.

HIGHER EDUCATION GOVERNANCE

The higher education governance system in Wisconsin was not a strong theme that emerged in this study, however, it must be addressed to provide context for use in comparison with Ohio and Georgia. As I stated briefly in the introduction to this case, Wisconsin operates a consolidated governing board that controls all thirteen campuses of the UW system. This system was established in 1971 with the merger of the University of Wisconsin and Wisconsin State University System. Under the Board of Regents, the UW System Administration (UWSA) is the supervising body that oversees state budgeting for the campuses.

Interviewees report that the system is generally working well to manage campuses and maintain discipline between them. Most said that UWSA is effective in preventing competition between the UW campuses, complimenting UWSA's role in determining funding priorities and representing institutional needs. In regard to leadership, UW System President Katherine Lyall is viewed as capable in her role of integrating the special needs of system campuses.

The absence of higher education governance as a strong theme explaining UW-Madison's funding situation suggests that the system is functioning well as it relates to relegating and monitoring the missions and operations of the campuses. The Ohio case demonstrated how a weak governance system can have a detrimental effect on the financial health of the research university. In comparison to OSU, UW benefits from a strong state system as it relates to maintaining a stable level of funding. This data suggests that governance has an important role in keeping budgets for research universities in check among the other public institutions in the state. The central difference may lie in the structure of the governing board—consolidated versus a coordinating board—which will be discussed in more detail in subsequent chapters.

SUMMARY

The case study of the State of Wisconsin and UW-Madison reveals an interesting cultural struggle between the state's historically strong commitment to supporting higher education and the conservative funding trend of the last decade. The current political agenda is focused on accommodating alternative needs that are seemingly more pressing and important to the public. The consequence is that these priorities are putting a squeeze on UW-Madison's budget.

But the story of state funding for UW-Madison is not solely political and historical. There is a great deal of evidence to suggest that the university has not done well in making the case for supporting itself. As it became clear by interviewees, UW-Madison seems to be creeping away from the outreach component that once earned it the love and respect of the Wisconsin public. As the institution's service to state seemingly erodes and declines, so does state funding. The voices of the legislators often implied this important correlation.

Among the many challenges regarding UW outreach, the university is not organized in a way to galvanize the disconnected public service efforts of its schools and colleges. It is because of the university's decentralized approach to outreach that the university is struggling to effectively provide a holistic message toward support for the institution at-large. The main consequence of the current organization is that the contributions of the UW are becoming lost as the legendary Wisconsin Idea continues to fade.

Looking at the strength of its past and present decline, one could reasonably argue that state appropriations for UW-Madison were once at a level of "higher than predicted support" but have since slipped to the category of "predicted" or moderate support. While further statistical analysis would have to be undertaken to test this hypothesis, the combination of political factors and institutional drift from the Wisconsin Idea points to significant decline in support since the early part of the century.

CHAPTER 6

The University of Georgia

INTRODUCTION

The State of Georgia enjoys a rich political and social history that dates make to the earliest days of this country's existence. The youngest of the 13 original colonies, Georgia was among the leaders in the drive for national independence during the American Revolution. It was in 1788 that Georgia became the fourth state to ratify the constitution and become part of the union (Encyclopedia Americana, 1995).

From its founding through the early 20th Century, Georgia's economy has been largely driven by the fertility of its farmland. Cotton has long been the state's dominant agricultural product, but the state is also widely known for its leadership in the peanut and peach industries. In recent years, poultry and livestock farming has also been placed on the forefront of Georgia's agricultural agenda, and on the coast, Georgia's shrimping industry brings in over $4 million dollars a year (Encyclopedia Americana, 1995).

But like many other states, Georgia's farming and fisheries gave way to the emergence of industrialization during the early-mid 1900s. Since that time, Georgia has led the nation in production of paper, textile products, and processed chicken. Today, Georgia is home to a growing number of high-tech industries. Because of its technological progress, metropolitan Atlanta boasts of being the "economic engine of the South."

As for the people in Georgia, the population of the state has historically been racially mixed. During the Civil War, the percentage of blacks and whites were almost even. But today, the state is a bit less diverse with the dominant group being white Protestants. African Americans constitute approximately 25 percent of the Georgia's population in the 1990s (Encyclopedia Americana, 1995).

Georgia has a rich political history, with much of it shaped by its role in the Civil War. The 5th state to join the Confederacy, Georgia was eventually decimated by Sherman's army in 1865. But out of the economic ruins of the period emerged a strong Democratic Party. The fact that Georgian's have not elected a republican governor for over 100 years is evidence that the party still is the dominant political force in the state. Throughout its history, Georgia has remained a relatively low tax state. Much of the state's general-purpose revenue is derived from sales tax, surtaxes on tobacco and fuels, and corporate and income taxes (Encyclopedia Americana, 1995).

The University of Georgia's roots go back to the early days following the American Revolution. Founded in 1785, UGA became the first state chartered university in the country. The charming southern town of Athens has been home to the campus since 1801. The early university curriculum focused on traditional classical studies, and later included law in 1843. In 1873, the curriculum was drastically expanded when the university became the state's land-grant institution under the Morrill Act. At that point, UGA broadened its curriculum to include courses in agriculture and mechanical arts. Today, thirteen schools and colleges carry out the University's mission of teaching, research, and public service (University of Georgia Website, 1999).

In 1999, the University of Georgia enrolls close to 29,000 undergraduate and graduate students, and offers affordable annual undergraduate tuition at $2,930 (University of Georgia Website, 1999). Unlike OSU and UW, UGA could be considered a "state supported" institution rather than a "state assisted" one. As Figure 6.1 points out, UGA's budget is heavily derived from state appropriations, with federal and private contacts considerably less a portion of the pie than UW especially. Accordingly, the expenditures reflect the state vs. national focus as research expenditures comprise 23.9 percent of the budget (compared to 31.9 at UW) and service to the state constitutes 13.5 percent (compared to 6.4 percent at UW and 4.5 percent at OSU).

Georgia's nationally acclaimed HOPE scholarship program offers free tuition for high school students who enter with a "B" average and maintain it throughout their enrollment at any public university in Georgia. Since 1931, the university has been governed by a consolidated governing board called the Board of Regents. The Board of Regents oversees the University System of Georgia which supervises all 35 institutions in the system.

A case study of the State of Georgia and the University of Georgia suggests a unique interdependency that exists between the two entities. Strong political support for the campus combined with a public knowledge and appreciation for the contributions of UGA and the University of System of Georgia explain the present strength of the state-university relationship, and subsequent state support for UGA. The case study suggests that three families of factors best explain the high level of state support for the University of Georgia. These are the political climate, UGA outreach and public service, and the higher education governance system.

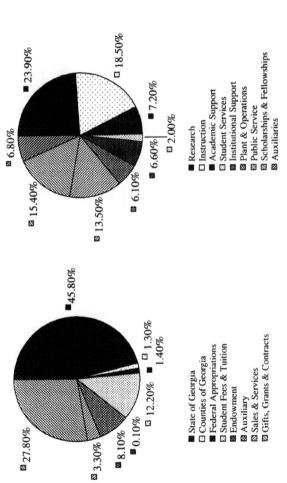

Source: UGA Factbook (1997). Office of Institutional Research and Planning, University of Georgia
http://www.uga.edu/Irp/fb97/09fin/09fintoc1.htm

Revenue by Source

Expenditures by Activity

- ■ Research
- □ Instruction
- ■ Academic Support
- ☒ Student Services
- ■ Institutional Support
- ☒ Plant & Operations
- ☒ Public Service
- ☒ Scholarships & Fellowships
- ☒ Auxiliaries

- ■ State of Georgia
- □ Counties of Georgia
- ■ Federal Appropriations
- ☒ Student Fees & Tuition
- ■ Endowment
- ☒ Auxiliary
- ☒ Sales & Services
- ☒ Gifts, Grants & Contracts

Figure 6.1. University of Georgia Budgeted Resources and Expenditurers (1996–97)

POLITICAL CLIMATE

Gubernatorial support and initiatives

The influence of former governor, Zell Miller, has clearly had a tremendous impact on state support for higher education in Georgia. Interviewees talked at length about how the governor led the charge in making higher education the number one priority during his six-year term in office (1991-1998). Interviewees suggest that one of Miller's motivations behind his support is the fact that Georgia has historically been ranked low in educational quality rankings. "What drove the Governor to support higher education is that we need an educated workforce in order to be a national center... the Governor recognized that we need to make up in some key areas, so higher education has become the centerpiece of his administration." Beyond the desire to catch up, interviewees suggest that higher education was a way that Governor Miller could best make a difference in Georgia. Said one interviewee, "Governor Miller spoke of his legacy and what he could do to make the most meaningful impact on the State. He felt that supporting higher education was the way to leave his mark."

During his term, Governor Miller led major high-profile education initiatives—the largest being the Georgia lottery to fund the HOPE scholarship program. The nationally recognized HOPE program allows all state high school graduates who earn a "B" average to be eligible for a tuition-free education at any Georgia public university for as long as that student retains a "B" average in college. Qualifying students may also choose to apply a portion of the tuition waiver to attend any private university in the state. Miller's speeches revealed that the goal of the program is to keep the brightest students in Georgia as a way to improve the state's economy and its residents' quality of life. After HOPE scholarship recipients are served, remaining lottery revenue is deposited into an equipment transfer fund, technology trust fund, and into libraries and construction to be used for higher education institutions.

Beyond these special programs, the Governor demonstrated strong support for faculty salary increases. In 1996, the Governor redirected 5 percent of all state agency budgets to fund a 6 percent increase in faculty salaries. Each campus redirected their own budgets toward the effort, using the savings to provide a 5 percent salary increase on their home campus. As expected, the governor's political support was extremely high in districts that are home to Georgia's public universities.

It is clear that Miller has made an enormous impact on placing higher education at the forefront of investment in the State of Georgia. Miller's rationale for supporting higher education was anchored in the long-term benefits that an educated citizenry would afford the state. In this case, higher education was viewed as an opportunity to create the future in the State of Georgia. The strong partnership that UGA and other state colleges and universities enjoy with the state can, in part, be credited to the vision and leadership of the Miller administration and the legislators that endorsed his plan.

Legislative Support, Priorities

After my interviews with state legislators, it became obvious that most were excited to stand behind the Governor's support for higher education because of its positive implications for the State. Said one member of the assembly, "The HOPE scholarship keeps our best students here... our reputation goes up, and it ultimately improves our tax base. It's just a positive cycle." Another added, "People in Georgia see the HOPE program as a way to improve their condition, it gives this generation a whole new attitude." Interviewees agree that the public has deeply embraced the program, which has virtually revolutionized the way Georgians think about higher education. Because of the HOPE scholarship, interviewees say that pursuing a college education is now viewed as less of a sacrifice, especially among residents in rural communities.

Similarly, the Governor's plan to redirect the budget for faculty salaries has been equally well supported by the legislature because it was promoted as a way to boost the state's economy. The theory is that salary increases allow Georgia institutions to attract, retain, and recruit the best faculty. In turn, faculty bring with them knowledge and high tech industry, which consequently boosts the state's economy. One interviewee summed it up, "The Governor sold the legislature on the idea that high-level faculty bring with them high tech jobs and better students. In the end it means an improvement in our economy and tax base."

Legislative support of Governor Miller's agenda has been critical to maintaining a culture of strong support for higher education in the State of Georgia. The legislators have clearly benefited politically from the Miller administration, as investment in higher education can be clearly marketed to constituents in all Georgia districts. Because the HOPE scholarship stands to serve all citizens in the state, it has earned the support of multiple constituencies in Georgia. Parents, students, and businesses all stand behind these efforts because of the potential it has to transform the economy and social structure of the state.

Politics and the Economy

The recession of early 1990's caused a brief blip in an otherwise strong decade of support for higher education in Georgia. However, Georgia now reports being the fast growing economy east of the Mississippi River, with high revenue growth, new jobs, and booming industry. The strong economy has allowed Georgia to invest heavily in higher education while cutting taxes and attending to the competing needs of the State. But overall, interviewees report that the strong economy is only one piece contributing to strong support for higher education in Georgia. Most point directly to the placement of priorities among Georgia's elected officials. Interviewees explain that the Governor and lawmakers view investing in higher education as a way to keep the economy strong. "The economy has been booming so we are encouraging the University to grow and bring in multi-million dollar businesses such as biotechnology" said one interviewee. "Investing in higher education is the way to keep the ball rolling." While interviewees noted that other problems will eventually demand the attention of state dollars such as crowding in jails, most agreed that the higher education priority prevails. One interviewee summed it up, "The economy is good, we're spending less on welfare now, and the lottery money helps fund education. But in the end, it's just a matter of priorities."

This last statement sheds light on an important issue as it relates to factors that influence levels of state support for higher education. As the literature review discussed in chapter two, the economy has a significant role in determining the level of state appropriations for postsecondary education institutions in the state. While this is true, the Georgia example suggests that political factors may be just as important. It is clear that political alliances in the state play an important role in keeping funding for higher education strong even in times of economic hardship. In other words, the strength of the partnership between higher education institutions and the state may be an important key to mitigating large fluctuations in university budgets based on economic conditions.

OUTREACH AND VISIBILITY

During my interviews, it quickly became evident that UGA's high visibility across the state has positively affected public attitudes toward the campus, and subsequently state support for the university. In general, three main factors have contributed to this visibility: the UGA outreach program, a visible president, and the institution's public service academic rank.

UGA Outreach Program

The University of Georgia operates a comprehensive outreach and public service program in keeping with its role as the state's land-grant university. Under the leadership of the Provost and Vice Chancellor for Public Service, the centralized unit oversees outreach activities in every Georgia County including small business development centers in 18 offices, and outreach coordinators in every school. Campus administrators reported that UGA faculty made over 300 outreach appearances in 1997. Among the many areas of outreach, UGA has helped with textile research, peanut farming, peach growing, shrimping, the poultry industry, and business development. In addition, the public affairs school is known as an important center that trains government leaders at the state, county and municipal level.

All interviewees agreed that the UGA outreach program has made a tremendous impact in gaining public support for the university. One state administrator told me about the far-reaching effects of UGA's outreach efforts, "UGA is seen as having people out in the community in response to them. The fact is that citizens feel that their lives have been enriched because of the outreach program." There is a general sense that UGA is living up to its charge as the land-grant institution, and because of it, legislative support for the institution has been strong. One legislator even claimed, "I dare not touch the funding for UGA outreach because the folks in my district depend on their expertise." This particular comment spoke to the strength of the program, suggesting that the outreach arm of the university has become so pervasive in Georgia communities that it has almost become entitlement. The implication is that the work of the university is highly supported because the benefits to state citizens are clear. Or as one interviewee summed it up, "Support for UGA is stable and broad because it is seen as fulfilling the land grant mission."

The success of the outreach program seems to be linked to the stability and strength of the formal structure that operates it. The Office of Outreach and Public Service operates a comprehensive communication program that effectively relays the UGA outreach messages to the public at-large. For example, the unit takes advantage of undergraduate service learning experiences to advertise the public service successes of the campus. In this program, journalism students produce an annual publication titled, *Impact*, that highlights the outreach activities of the university. The publication, which is sent to all members of the general assembly and every high school, promotes the campus while providing valuable experience for the students. Said one UGA official, "The publication, *Impact*, has gotten a lot of attention across the State. It gives our students real-life experience and allows them to become our PR agents."

UGA's commitment to public service and outreach has clearly paid large dividends as it relates to leveraging support for the institution. The structure and dollars behind UGA's outreach efforts have sent a strong message to the state about the institution's priorities. UGA has been a responsive partner attending to the needs of the state and in turn, the state has reciprocated its support for the institution. The public service career ladder is an example of a structure built to reinforce UGA's commitment to outreach and engagement.

Public Service Academic Rank

Supporting its outreach initiative, the University of Georgia has adopted an alternative public service career ladder, which encourages faculty to focus on matters of public concern. Faculty that join this program focus primarily on the public-policy needs of the state. They have direct contact with citizens and officials in their own environment and are involved with state and local leaders in the areas of educational needs assessment, program development, training, consultation, and technical assistance. Individuals are promoted in a ranking system similar to traditional faculty ranks—from the public service assistant to the senior public service associate. This career track is growing in prominence, as there are now 800 UGA faculty members on this program. Legislators and other state officials report that this program is well recognized and highly regarded.

In addition to this alternative career ladder, faculty in traditional tenure track system are now expected to be more serious in their pursuit of public service. Said one UGA official, "It used to be that research was the main driver in promotion decisions. Now it's important to show success in at least two of the three areas: teaching, research, or public service. Public service has certainly become a more important criteria." The UGA administrator explained that placing importance on public service requires a change in philosophy and can only work if it emanates from the top.

Visible President

Most interviewees reported that the visibility of UGA's President has helped the University gain public support. The President makes high-profile trips to outreach stations, research centers, and community organizations to show his support for Georgia's local communities. In particular, a trip to the coast made a statement about President Adam's interest in helping industry in the state. The media coverage for the event showed the President appearing on a fishing boat in an attempt to understand the needs of Georgia's shrimping industry.

The President's support for outreach stands as a symbol of the institution's commitment to the state. As forthcoming sections will discuss, the appearance of the president must be accompanied by action to demonstrate the depth of the service that the institution provides. In the case of UGA, President Adam's appearance accurately reflects the work of the multiple service units that are deployed throughout the state. This "truth in advertising" is critically important as it relates to building institutional credibility.

UGA Tradition

UGA's visibility can largely be attributed to its prominence in outreach, but independent of its success in this area, most interviewees confessed that UGA has a natural niche' of support because the institution has long been regarded as the state's flagship university. The institution's distinction as being the oldest state chartered university in the United States contributes to the deep loyalty felt by multiple generations of UGA alumni who encourage their children to follow the family tradition. Most interviewees agreed that the University of Georgia is viewed as state residents' first choice for public higher education.

However, this deep loyalty is in jeopardy among some Georgia families. Since the focus at UGA has been on quality rather than expanded volumes of students, enrollments have been cut while admission standards have risen. The result of scaling back enrollment is that the children of some alumni can't get into the University. One interviewee explained the dilemma, "In some cases there have been three or four generations of Georgia families who have attended the University. The problem occurs when all of a sudden the next generation can't get in. This has led to an erosion in support in some circles." On the other hand, it is reported that the focus on quality has increased public loyalty because it has sent a message to the most talented Georgia students that it is legitimate to attend the University of Georgia as opposed to attending neighboring UNC-Chapel Hill. As the Wisconsin case pointed out, UW-Madison has faced similar problems with its enrollment management plan. Although problems such as these threaten political support for institutions, they are combated by alliances who concentrate their efforts on increasing quality, even if it compromises access to the institution.

HIGHER EDUCATION GOVERNANCE

Georgia is similar to Wisconsin in that it operates a system of 35 campuses under a consolidated governing board. Interviewees agreed that the University System of Georgia is effective in meeting the overall needs of higher education in the state. Most important, the interviewees suggested that the System, under the leadership of the Chancellor, has helped each of the institutions develop distinct missions and a collaborative environment so that all institutions benefit from each other. The Governor's support for the 6 percent salary increase at every Georgia campus, along with library improvements throughout the system affirmed the System's philosophy.

The leadership of the USG Chancellor, Stephen Portch, has clearly had an impact on strengthening the relationship between the University System of Georgia and the State. First, the Chancellor's proactive stance on accountability has sent the message that the USG plans to be good stewards of the public money it is appropriated. The annual accountability report, created by the Chancellor for the Governor and general assembly, summarizes the use of all state money directed for specific educational programs. Interviewees report that this has been well received by the administration. Said one interviewee from system administration, "We recognized that the System should have its house in order if we expect to get support from [the state]. We can't just expect [the Governor and legislature] to leave the money on the stump."

In addition, interviewees report that Chancellor Portch and the Governor have a good working relationship and most often "speak with one voice." Working closely with the Governor, the Chancellor has been very aggressive in his approach to meeting the economic needs of the State. Interviewees said that attending to economic needs was once more of an institutional activity, but now it is a System activity. UGA campus officials report that the Chancellor's initiatives are complimentary to UGA initiatives and are aimed to draw out the strengths of each system campus.

Special Programs Tied to Economic Development

Two special USG system initiated economic development programs have bridged the work of Georgia public universities and the private sector. These programs are the Intellectual Capital Partnership Program (ICAPP) and the Georgia Research Alliance. Interviewees report that these two initiatives have had a significant impact on levels of state support for public universities in Georgia, including UGA.

Intellectual Capital Partnership Program (ICAPP)

In 1995, the Georgia legislature created a University System of Georgia, Office of Development and Economic Services to leverage the vast resources of the state's 34 public colleges and universities on behalf of Georgia's economic development. From this office, the Intellectual Capital Partnership Program (ICAPP) was created. The ICAPP program was initiated with a statewide needs assessment to determine the educational and training needs for employees in high-quality, high-growth knowledge-based industries. Once determined, the University System compared the needs with the numbers of graduates produced in these areas to help the Board of Regents decide which programs should be created or expanded. These programs were identified and continue to be developed or expanded in Georgia public colleges and universities. The ICAPP program is credited with retaining and attracting top businesses such as Total Systems Services (TSS), a major information card processing center that reported revenues of $361.5 million in 1997. Interviewees explained that the ICAPP program helped to keep TSS in Georgia, and the company has since committed a capital investment of $100 million and plans to employ up to 5,000 new people.

Georgia Research Alliance

The Georgia Research Alliance represents a partnership between Georgia's public and private research universities, state government, and corporate partners. The purpose of the Alliance is to escalate the research capabilities of Georgia's research universities as a way to improve Georgia's economic future. The Alliance website explains that they hope to achieve critical mass or an emergence of a large enough pool of scientific entrepreneurs to lead to the rapid creation of start-up companies in the State. The Alliance reports that achieving this goal requires cutting edge research, a supportive business environment, skilled manpower, and adequate suppliers and customers. The Alliance is focusing on three specific research niches: advanced communications, environmental technologies, and biotechnology.

Since its inception in 1990, the Georgia Research Alliance has raised more than $200 million through a combination of state and private sources. These funds are used to attract and support eminent scholars and research facilities. Interviewees report that the Alliance has significantly helped to bring state and private support to the research universities in the state, and that the success of this venture stands to benefit everyone. Said one supportive interviewee, "The Georgia Research Alliance enhances everyone—it boosts existing industries and brings top scholars and new development to Georgia."

The economic development initiatives advanced by the University System of Georgia have demonstrated a clear commitment to serving the future needs of the state. UGA and a host of Georgia campuses are important partners in executing the plan and receive strong support to accomplish economic goals. This case suggests that the USG's innovation has been catalytic in strengthening the partnership between the state and its public colleges and universities. As the state's flagship university, the University of Georgia is poised to provide a leadership role in advancing these directives advanced by the USG. This visibility further serves to link UGA as an important entity shaping the future of the state.

SUMMARY

The case study points to some important reasons why the University of Georgia is highly supported by the state. Most important, Governor Zell Miller's term in office has made a colossal impact on the state's inclination to support higher education and the UGA campus. One could argue that Miller's HOPE scholarship program has single-handedly changed Georgia's view of higher education. Once seen as only for the wealthy, the program has opened the door wide to all qualified Georgians seeking higher education opportunities. The University of Georgia has benefited greatly from the HOPE scholarship because Georgia's best and brightest students now flood the campus.

But the case study suggests that Miller's efforts were not just a gift to the State residents, but a vote of confidence in the University System of Georgia and UGA campus. The innovation and leadership within the System seems to have earned the investment, as it has sent a clear message that its primary goal is to keep the Georgia economy strong and residents' quality of life high. The well regarded ICAPP program is convincing evidence of USG's commitment to these efforts in step with the objectives set forth by the governor and legislature.

Accordingly, state and public support for UGA is high because the campus is tremendously successful in fulfilling its land-grant mission. The case study suggests that the visibility of the campus pervades all areas of the state including schools, industry, and agriculture. The unique public service track is likely to be a large reason behind this success because of its rigorous focus on community needs assessment and delivery of instruction. The formal structure called the *Office for Outreach and Public Service* seems to aid this effort a great deal. The Office not only provides coordination and stability of these efforts, but also effectively gets the word out about the campuses commitment to the State. Finally, a supportive and visible president has helped UGA articulate its mission to important constituencies across the state.

CHAPTER 7

Cross-Case Analysis

CASE STUDY COMPARISON AND CONCEPTUAL FRAMEWORK

The case studies demonstrate that a complex array of state-institutional relation-ships play an important role in shaping state support for research institutions. Table 7.1 summarizes these relationships matched against my conceptual framework outlined in chapter two. The purpose of the table is to add structure to the themes that emerged in the cases and provide a side-by-side review of each critical piece of evidence as they compare to the other states and institutions investigated. This "compare and contrast" format provides a framework for the narrative cross-case analysis presented in the sections that follow. Overall, this chapter examines the evidence and advance conclusions about factors that appear to be most useful for explaining the varying levels of state support for the three institutions.

Table 7.1 Comparison of Case Study States and Institutions

	Higher than Predicted Appropriations	Predicted Appropriations	Lower than Predicted Appropriations
	State of Georgia, University of Georgia	*State of Wisconsin, University of Wisconsin-Madison*	*State of Ohio, The Ohio State University*
1. Economic/fiscal policy factors			
State economic health and effect on higher education appropriations	Recession of early 90s caused a blip in strong support for higher education. Now, fast growing economy: high revenue growth, new jobs, industry. Increased investment in higher ed seen as the way to continue this growth.	Recession of early 90s caused steady reduction in higher ed funding. Now, strong economy, budget surpluses used for property tax relief, lower taxes, other priorities. Higher ed. Appropriations not increased with economic recovery.	Recession of early 90s resulted in large cuts in higher ed spending. From 1990-95, OSU took biggest cut among Big 10 peers. As economy recovers, higher education funding increasing as a way to catch up from past budgets.
Taxes	Low tax state	High tax state	Low tax state
2. Political Factors:			
Gubernatorial priorities, support, impressions of the campus.	Higher ed and economic development is centerpiece of Gov. Zell Millers administration. Developed lottery to fund HOPE scholars, h.e. capital needs. Supports faculty salary increases, special initiatives. All tied to economic development.	Gov. Thompsons priority is K-12 school refinancing and property tax relief, corrections, lower taxes. Educational concentration on K-12, technology, job training. Gov supports high profile UW initiatives. Relations with UW perceived as not strong.	Efficiency and accountability issues strained Govs Voinovich relationship with OSU in early 1990s. Gov seen as more supportive of 2 yr. schoolsseen as more practical. K-12, corrections, human services high priority for Gov.

Legislative priorities, support, impressions of the campus.	Leg supports Gov. Because HOPE scholarship/ fac salaries, higher ed support seen as keeping kids in Georgia, brings in high tech jobs, expands tax base, improving economy. UGA outreach is visible, valued in all districtsthus leg. sees UGA as worthy of support.	K-12, property tax relief, tax cuts, corrections are main priorities. Some leg. view UW as ungrateful, elitist, irrelevant research not helping state solve problems, some accountability failures.	Educational focus on K-12, also two-year schools. Leg. mostly concerned about support for campus in their district. OSU is seen as big, elitist, lack of faculty interaction and commitment to public service. Push for Ohio BOR to look at vision of higher ed for entire State.
3. Governance of Higher Education:			
Model/Structure of Higher Education Governance in the State: perceived strength of the structure	Consolidated governing board: Univ. System of Georgia. Structure viewed as useful for coordinating, planning for h.e. needs of the State. Institutional missions seen as distinct, complimentary. All have important role.	Consolidated governing board: UW System Administration. In general, system viewed as working well to manage campuses, maintain discipline, prevent competition between campuses.	Coordinating board: Ohio Board of Regents. Campus missions viewed as competitive, duplicative, but improving with recent BOR initiatives. Since 1997, BOR taken a stronger role in planning h.e. needs of the State.
Authority Relationships and Leadership: System/Campus/ State	System Chancellor viewed as strong, innovative. Governor and Chancellor viewed as speaking with one voice.	UW System President viewed as effective in integrating special needs of system campuses. Relations between UW Chancellor and Gov. perceived as not strong.	Historically loose authority relationship between Ohio BOR and campusesstrength of metro campuses make it difficult to unify. Gov originally skeptical of OSU due to accountability issues.

Governing Board initiatives affecting support for campuses	Intellectual Capital Partnership Program (ICAPP) to link campuses with economic development. Cooperative with Georgia Research Alliance	Board primarily plays the role of determining funding priorities and representing institutional needs. Board innovation was not a theme in this study.	1995 Higher Education Funding Commissionstrate gic plan for higher education funding in the State and Managing for the Future task force well received by legislature.
4. Cultural Factors:			
State citizens value accorded to higher education	HOPE Scholarship credited with raising citizens value for higher educationhigher ed now viewed as less of a sacrifice especially in rural communities.	Historically high value accorded to higher educationlong standing values of quality, access, and affordability.	Ohio historically prosperous in manufacturing/indus try, created culture that college not necessary for advancement. Thus, feeling that burden of cost should be on users.
Campus visibility and state citizens collective value accorded to the campus.	Oldest chartered institution in USA results in long standing loyalty to UGA, multi-generational alumni have deep support. UGA valued across State due to highly visible outreach programcampus seen as fulfilling UGAs land-grant mission/solving States problems.	Public, parents of students are proud of UW quality, high rankings, quality of UW grads recognized. General public largely unaware of UWs impact beyond educating state- seen as a limited partner in economic development and public service.	OSU less recognized across state because citizens and legislators have strongest allegiance to their regional campuses. Overall, OSU not widely viewed or spoken as flagship campus. OSUs football team well known and regarded across the State. Ag school seen has fulfilling land-grant mission, but others not.

	Higher than Predicted Appropriations	Predicted Appropriations	Lower than Predicted Appropriations
	State of Georgia, University of Georgia	*State of Wisconsin, University of Wisconsin-Madison*	*State of Ohio, The Ohio State University*
Influence of campus CEO	President visible through visits with industries, urban and rural communities across the State. President viewed as having outreach/business focus.	Chancellor never cited as having an effect one way or the other on influencing State support for UW. A campus perception exists that Gov/Chanc relationship is not strong.	Former President, Gordon Gee cited as improving visibility of OSU across the State. Gee viewed as having strong outreach, business community focus.
Campus commitment to Public Service	Public service career track well supported by UGA top admins, Interviewees say UGA demonstrates its support for the State.	Service to State seen as not rewarded, faculty unknown to community and some research viewed as irrelevant. Wisconsin Idea called a lost notion.	Service to State seen as not rewarded or valued in OSU campus culture and administration.
University Relations Structure	Formal structure, VP for University Relations oversees all UR relations activities on campus.	Decentralized, informal University Relations Team serves to communicate, coordinate efforts across campus.	Decentralized, informal Outreach and Engagement Council serves to communicate, coordinate efforts across campus.
Outreach and Public Service Structure	Formal, centralized structure: Office of Outreach and Public Service manages, publicizes all outreach activities across State.	Decentralized, schools and colleges operate own outreach activities. UW Extension campus most responsible for outreach.	Decentralized, schools and colleges operate own outreach activities.

	Higher than Predicted Appropriations	**Predicted Appropriations**	**Lower than Predicted Appropriations**
	State of Georgia, University of Georgia	*State of Wisconsin, University of Wisconsin-Madison*	*State of Ohio, The Ohio State University*
5. Institutional Characteristics and Strategies			
Tuition policy	Low tuition: HOPE scholarship provides full tuition for Georgia B average high school graduates who maintain a B average at any public Georgia university. HOPE also provides assistance with Georgia private schools	Low tuition: Growing sentiment to raise tuition due to competing needs of the state and feeling that the quality of the institution necessitates higher tuition. This view is divided among legislators.	High tuition: General feeling that higher education mostly benefits the students, so tuition should be higher. In general, no public push to change this policy, but Ohio BOR beginning to make it an issue.
Institutional strategies used to Gain state support	UGA President visits across State. Wide distribution of service learning/outreach journal viewed as having an impact. Other publications, cultivating relationships with legislatures.	Publications, state relations plan to show campus impact, establish relationships with leg/state citizens and alums. Campus visits by legislators, recognition of UW advocates	Trying to link to economic development, send the message that h.e. is important for future work force, publications, improving retention, instruction quality to boost image, pushing performance funding as a way to show tangible results.

	Higher than Predicted Appropriations	**Predicted Appropriations**	**Lower than Predicted Appropriations**
	State of Georgia, University of Georgia	*State of Wisconsin, University of Wisconsin-Madison*	*State of Ohio, The Ohio State University*
Influence of campus CEO	President visible through visits with industries, urban and rural communities across the State. President viewed as having outreach/business focus.	Chancellor never cited as having an effect one way or the other on influencing State support for UW. A campus perception exists that Gov/Chanc relationship is not strong.	Former President, Gordon Gee cited as improving visibility of OSU across the State. Gee viewed as having strong outreach, business community focus.
Campus commitment to Public Service	Public service career track well supported by UGA top admins, Interviewees say UGA demonstrates its support for the State.	Service to State seen as not rewarded, faculty unknown to community and some research viewed as irrelevant. Wisconsin Idea called a lost notion.	Service to State seen as not rewarded or valued in OSU campus culture and administration.
University Relations Structure	Formal structure, VP for University Relations oversees all UR relations activities on campus.	Decentralized, informal University Relations Team serves to communicate, coordinate efforts across campus.	Decentralized, informal Outreach and Engagement Council serves to communicate, coordinate efforts across campus.
Outreach and Public Service Structure	Formal, centralized structure: Office of Outreach and Public Service manages, publicizes all outreach activities across State.	Decentralized, schools and colleges operate own outreach activities. UW Extension campus most responsible for outreach.	Decentralized, schools and colleges operate own outreach activities.

The case studies and comparison table makes it clear that each institution and state has its own unique political, institutional, and socio-economic history that is largely responsible for shaping present-day investment in higher education. While the complexities of these factors make it difficult to pinpoint exact determinants of state support, a few main themes clearly emerged as being important. As the forthcoming sections explain, each of these critical themes were also supported by the findings of the regression analysis. The purpose of this chapter is to closely examine these themes and demonstrate their magnitude through a comparison of the three case studies. Beyond the presentation of the main themes, key factors identified in my conceptual framework that did not surface as important determinants will also be discussed, as they provide equally valuable clues about the relative weight of various elements in explaining differences in state support for research universities.

Overall, the case studies supported three main factors to explain the differences in state support for the research universities during the 1990s: campus commitment to outreach and public service, strength of the higher education governance system, and the extent of gubernatorial support. In other words, state support for research universities is largely contingent on the actions and commitment of three critical entities: the campus, the higher education governance structure, and state government.

THE CAMPUS

Commitment to Public Service

The regression analysis from this study suggested that greater state appropriations for research universities are highly correlated with institutional expenditures on public service. Stated another way, the deeper campus commitment to public service in dollars, the greater state support for the institution. The case studies of UGA, UW and OSU supported this finding, and further asserted that the visibility of public service activities is a critical element in garnering state appropriations for research universities.

As a percentage of total expenditures, UGA spends significantly more on public service and outreach than does UW and OSU. As the pie charts in chapter four illustrated, during the 1996-97 fiscal year, 13.5 percent of UGA's budget was allocated for these activities compared to 4.5 percent at OSU and 6.4 percent at UW. The differences in the outreach budget for each of the three campuses seems to mirror the success of the programs. The variation in the public's knowledge of the three programs is wide, and can be largely attributed to institutional differences in commitment to public service, structure of the public service function, depth of operation, and marketing/communication of the program.

Of these elements, the best evidence of differences in commitment to public service can be seen in the variation of institutional rewards among the three campuses. At OSU and UW, most interviewees felt that public service is simply not a part of the institutional culture and priories for the institution, and not rewarded by the campuses. The example of the OSU faculty member who excelled as a public servant but was denied tenure was held up as blatant evidence of the institution's lack of commitment to this ideal. At UW, interviewees agreed that the virtues of the Wisconsin Idea are ultimately a low priority, and that the century-old concept has lost its flare.

Meanwhile UGA's alternative public service career ladder has put institutional commitment behind the public service component of its mission. Again, faculty members joining this program are rewarded and promoted in a ranking system similar to traditional faculty ranks. Throughout my interviews with Georgia officials, it became clear that the 800 UGA faculty members on this program have boosted the institution's public profile tremendously. Because of the institutional backing for this arrangement, UGA's commitment to outreach is widely known and highly regarded by legislators and the public at-large.

Another important difference to consider is the structure and organization of outreach at the three institutions. UGA's centralized approach to outreach has been an effective means to coordinate and promote all campus public service activities. On the other hand, UW and OSU's decentralized approach has seemingly hurt the two institutions. Interviewees talked at length about the difficulties of coordinating and promoting outreach when no clearinghouse for this type of information exists. As a researcher investigating outreach at the campuses, this point became even more apparent to me. At UGA, I received prompt attention and thorough information about public service with the help of the Office for Public Service and Outreach. At UW and OSU, it was significantly more difficult to retrieve the same type of information because I was constantly shuffled between a number of offices to develop a general sense of service activities across the institution. The strength of the centralized approach quickly became obvious to me as I directly benefited from the information clearinghouse at UGA.

To summarize, the study suggests that outreach activities at both UW and OSU are significantly less known and revered by government officials in Ohio and Wisconsin than UGA's outreach efforts in Georgia. An important conclusion is that the visibility and structure of public service is critical as it pertains to garnering state support for research universities—especially land grant institutions. Moreover, the effectiveness in sharing this message with the public is paramount. Sturdy, recognizable structures set up to coordinate and clearly communicate these initiatives to the public are seemingly a critical element in the success of these ventures.

Accountability

The case studies brought to life the importance of accountability and its implications for understanding support for research universities. Interestingly, interviewees from the legislature broadened the definition of accountability beyond the usual discussion of efficiency to focus on the outcomes of the work being done on campus. For example, interviewees in Ohio and Wisconsin stated that it was unclear about how "in-touch" the faculty are with the needs of the people in these states. Added to this view is an impression that many faculty don't work as hard as they should—and often not working hard enough on the right things. From this standpoint, it is clear that the accountability issue goes hand-in-hand with the aforementioned discussion about public service. The impact of the institution's work on the quality of life of state residents seems to be the ultimate measure of accountability.

But efficient and appropriate use of funds is also important. Governor Thompson's *Task Force on Accountability* recommended that the UW System report its progress in seven key areas: access, quality, effectiveness, efficiency, diversity, stewardship of assets, and contribution to compelling state needs. In Ohio, former Governor Voinovich established similar requirements for institutions in that state. In both states there remains a strong contingent of legislators and state officials that believe that both UW and OSU must do more to be efficient and accountable for use of state tax dollars.

In Georgia, the State University of Georgia Systems Chancellor's volunteered the creation of an accountability report as a way to win the respect of the Governor and legislators in that state. Interviewees report that this proactive stance was well received by the administration and state legislators. But more than this savvy measure by the system CEO, Georgia legislators told me that the comprehensive public service program remains the best evidence of UGA's accountability to the needs of Georgia residents.

In sum, accountability in terms of costs and efficiencies is important, but should ultimately be defined in terms of outcomes and service. As one Ohio legislator put it, "Showing cost efficiencies is important, but demonstrating that our School of Education has improved local schools is even more valuable."

HIGHER EDUCATION GOVERNANCE

Management and Coordination

The statistical analysis suggests that research universities governed under a consolidated board system are likely to receive higher appropriations than those research institutions in coordinating board systems or planning and service agencies. The causes behind this finding were animated throughout the case studies.

UGA and UW operate under single governance systems managed by the University System of Georgia and the University of Wisconsin System, respectively. Interviewees suggested that both systems are strong and effective in planning for the research university and for the higher education needs of the state. Although it did not emerge as a key indicator of state support, the UW System was generally cited as a stable system that has worked well to manage campuses, maintain discipline, and prevent competition between campuses. The University System of Georgia was often discussed as being strong, innovative and useful for coordinating and planning for the higher education needs of the State. Like Wisconsin, institutional missions at Georgia public universities are generally regarded as distinct and complimentary.

But an analysis of Ohio revealed a different story. Interviewees noted the historical strength of the metro areas in the state has made it difficult to unify higher education in Ohio. Because Ohio is more of a collection of large cities, or "city states" having strong commitments to their regional or metro universities, institutions have historically had less regard for viewing overall state needs. The coordinating board system—the Ohio Board of Regents—was often cited as being weak in its attempt to reconcile and coordinate the missions of these institutions.

An important conclusion is that research universities appear to be financially healthier when they are part of a strong university system and under the authority of a consolidated governing board. In these systems, research institutions are recognized has having a unique role within the overall picture of higher education in the state as opposed to having competitive relationships with other state campuses. In Georgia and Wisconsin, for example, UGA and UW are widely recognized as the flagship campus holding the role as the state problem solver and economic generator. At OSU the land grant role is seemingly diffused among a number of neighboring institutions. In this case, the institution must constantly compete to maintain its place among other campuses. This study suggests that consolidated governing boards help research universities maintain their unique niche' because the boards have greater authority to control the activities of all state campuses. In other words, these types of boards have more success in planning for the state's higher education needs as a whole, resulting in more equitable distribution of resources for all campuses and better stewardship of state dollars.

Economic Development Focus

The case studies also suggest that a system-wide focus on the economic development needs of the state is critical to garnering support for research universities. The findings are backed by the aforementioned literature suggesting that university systems and institutions that clearly demonstrate and effectively communicate a commitment to economic development are likely to receive higher support from their states.

Again, the case study of Georgia provides a good example of economic development innovation at the system level. The University System of Georgia's Intellectual Capital Partnership Program (ICAPP), has been credited with retaining and attracting top businesses to Georgia and forging strong partnerships between public and private universities and local communities in the state. Interviewees suggest that state legislators recognize the value of these programs and financially support it because it is clearly linked to economic benefits. The visible success of these endeavors has distinctly strengthened the relationship between the state and universities, and subsequently the funding stream between the state and USG.

Conversely, innovation among the higher education governance structures in Ohio and Wisconsin were considerably less obvious than Georgia. Put simply, the activities of these structures seemed much less proactive and visionary as compared to USG and its ICAPP program. In Wisconsin and Ohio, the governing structure's focus seems largely directed towards managing the campuses as opposed to leveraging the resources of the institutions toward a specific outcome. While the message of economic development underlies the rhetoric of the Ohio Board of Regents and UW System, it is not clear that the governing bodies are actually doing anything to achieve these goals. As a researcher, I sense that the two systems are relying on their institutions to carry out the broadly defined goals of economic development. Innovation at the governance level seems to be an important piece of following through with the message about higher education's commitment to ensuring a healthy state economy.

STATE GOVERNMENT

Gubernatorial Support

The statistical analysis revealed that the state political climate has a significant impact on levels of support for research universities. In particular, public universities residing in states where Democrats control both the upper and lower house of the legislature are likely to have greater unrestricted appropriations. The case study supported this finding, but reinforced the literature suggesting that governors may have the strongest political impact on support for higher education.

For example, the case study of Georgia clearly shows that former Governor Zell Miller had a colossal impact on placing higher education as the top priority in the state. In fact, it could be argued that the HOPE scholarship program and plan to redirect the budget for faculty salaries could only have survived with gubernatorial support.

Meanwhile, recent governors in Wisconsin and Ohio have placed a number of competing state initiatives in front of higher education. Prior to the 1999 biannual budget, Wisconsin Governor Tommy Thompson's agenda focused primarily on K-12 financing, corrections, and tax cuts—themes that have been consistent throughout his 8 years in office. Like Wisconsin, former Ohio Governor George Voinovich focused on K-12 reform, corrections, Medicare, and tax cuts throughout his term in the 1990s. Voinovich was more supportive of the two-year college system than higher education because he viewed technical schools as a more direct link to helping business and industry in the State.

In sum, this study shows that during the early to mid-1990s, higher education was viewed as a secondary priority in Wisconsin and Ohio, while a top priority in Georgia. From this analysis, it is clear that gubernatorial influence is a crucial indicator of state support for higher education.

The Economy

The literature suggests that the economic health of a state is an important determinant of state support for higher education. But evidence from this study suggests that the current politics of the state may be a better predictor than any economic indicator. For instance, Wisconsin, Ohio, and Georgia have all enjoyed healthy economies throughout the late 1990s, however, elected officials in each state have simply chosen to spend additional resources differently. Miller directed much of the additional revenue toward higher education, whereas Thompson and Voinovich used the revenue cushion to pursue other priorities.

A look back at the early half of the 1990s strengthens this argument. At that time, the majority of the states in the U.S. were feeling the effects of a difficult recession. Interviewees from Georgia, Ohio, and Wisconsin all reported their financial struggles during this difficult period. In fact, all three states scaled back on their investment in higher education during the early 1990s. But the difference lies in level of cuts taken by each of the institutions. In Ohio, higher education was cut drastically. Ohio State University took the largest cuts among its peer institutions in the Big Ten. The UW-Madison budget was also reduced quite significantly in the early 1990s, and has been the slowest to recover among all of the Big Ten universities. However, Georgia interviewees reported that the recession of the early 1990s resulted in only a brief blip in support for higher education, which quickly rebounded. Furthermore, the regression analysis in this study demonstrates that Georgia was providing more appropriations than one would expect, even during this tough economic period (1991-92 database). These observations lead to the conclusion that state politics takes precedent over the health of the economy when determining state appropriations for higher education.

State History and Culture

Do history and culture make an important difference in determining state appropriations for research universities? The answer is yes and no. In Ohio, the historical cultural strength of the blue-collar economy is clearly keeping investment in higher education at a modest level. Administrators at Ohio State University talked at length about their difficult task of educating the public about the merits of investment in higher education—changing the public's philosophy that higher education is still a luxury. History and culture are definitely important factors precluding greater investment in Ohio's higher education system.

On the other hand, Wisconsin's rich history and culture has not necessarily guaranteed it great support for the present and future. Support for UW would have likely been in the "more than predicted" category fifteen years ago. However, the conservative trend in funding can be largely attributed to political and philosophical shifts of the last ten years. But beyond these emerging ideologies, this drift can also be attributed to institutional backsliding. As the case study pointed out, UW-Madison is no longer widely regarded as doing its part to help the state solve its problems. The combination of these factors has seemingly eroded the history of strong support for higher education in Wisconsin.

But the Georgia example shows how history and politics can change state culture on the positive side. Compared to other states, the quality of Georgia's education system always lagged behind its peers. But this not-so-flattering piece of Georgia's history is now being used to spur Georgians to "catch up" with other states. In this case, a less affirmative educational history has actually *improved* the higher education budget in the state. One interviewee from the USG explained that increased investment in higher education is seen as starting a new chapter in Georgia's history, helping to create the "New South." The HOPE scholarship, for example, has single-handedly changed Georgian's attitude about higher education—breathing new life into the public higher education system. Interviewees agreed that there is a genuine excitement about the changes in Georgia, and one participant noted that legislators are more excited to bring about major cultural improvements than having the less visionary task of maintaining an already strong culture. This profound point may also shed light on reasons behind the lagging support for the historically well-supported UW-Madison.

This chapter outlined the important elements that emerged as critical to understanding differences in state support for the campuses investigated. In chapter eight, I advance overall conclusions and present a framework for renewing the partnership between state governments and research universities.

Because of the important policy and strategy implications of this study, a section will be devoted to providing recommendations for campus administrators and policy-makers as they plan for the future of higher education in their states. To ground the conclusions in theory, the organizational theory framework will be reintroduced as a way to conceptually understand what was learned in the study. In the end, I will address important aspects of this study that merit additional research and consideration. This final section will provide new pathways of inquiry that build on the findings and conclusions of this study.

CHAPTER 8

A Framework for a Renewed Partnership

SUMMARY OF CONCLUSIONS

Both the quantitative and qualitative analysis of this study offer some important conclusions about factors essential to understanding differences in state support for research universities. The purpose of this section is to synthesize and summarize the conclusions derived from the study, and set the stage for examining strategies and policies for garnering greater state support for research universities.

Before these final conclusions are advanced, is important to explain that the contrasts between factors will often be presented in two categories: high support for UGA and low support for UW and OSU. While the regression model placed UW in the predicted support category, the strong political and institutional factors that emerged at UW largely mirrored those of OSU, making it difficult to distinguish between a moderate-low support category. This study suggests that the historically strong support for UW has not yet eroded to the point that the campus falls in the "less than predicted support." However, the similarity between Ohio and Wisconsin's political and OSU/UW institutional factors lead them to be treated in the same category for much of this analysis. For this reason, these two states and institutions are often lumped together in one moderate-low classification.

Given this caveat, the quantitative and qualitative analysis mutually supported three main factors to explain the differences in state support for research universities during the 1990s. First, institutional characteristics are crucial to understanding variations in support for research institutions. In the regression analysis, enrollment, revenue, and expenditures were all shown to be the model's most important predictors of unrestricted appropriations. But while the majority of these predictors are logical and expected, an institution's commitment to public service clearly stood out as a particularly critical factor in the qualitative component of this study. Interviewees at each of the three institutions gave varying accounts about the success of their outreach efforts and their implications for garnering state support for their particular campus. UGA's centralized approach and public service rank has earned it high marks, while UW and OSU's decentralized efforts are clearly less regarded and known by their elected officials and public at-large. The case studies suggest that the success of these efforts is critical to developing positive relationships with state governments and the general public. In sum, this study suggests that the level of state appropriations is linked with the visibility and success of these efforts.

Second, the findings from my analysis suggest that higher education governance plays a vital role in funding for research campuses. The regression model indicated that research I universities governed by a consolidated governing board are more likely to have higher appropriations than those governed by a coordinating board or planning and service agency. The case studies backed this finding, suggesting that the differences in support exist because consolidated governing boards have more control over the operation and missions of campuses, and thus more power to equitably allocate state dollars to the institutions.

Third, this study suggests that politics is an equally compelling factor to consider in an analysis of state funding for research institutions. In particular, research universities are likely to have higher appropriations in states where Democrats control both the senate and assembly. The case studies strengthened this observation, as Democrats dominated Georgia's upper and lower house of the legislature throughout the 1990s. On the other hand, Republicans commanded the Ohio and Wisconsin legislature during the budget creation during the early part of the 1990s, although they partially gave way to Democratic majorities during the later part of this decade (1996-1997).

The case studies animated the importance of the political influence of elected officials as evidenced by the varying priorities of the governors and legislators in the three states. In particular, the leadership of the governor emerged as the most important political influence. Governor Miller in Georgia placed higher education as a top priority while Thompson and Voinovich pursued other goals in Wisconsin and Ohio. The political affiliations of the governors in these states also reflect a party division as suggested by the regression model: Miller is a Democrat and Thompson and Voinovich are Republicans.

An important economic indicator closely relating to politics and culture, is the effect of the tax rate on state support. For every additional dollar in taxes collected per capita, the regression model predicted an additional $43.6 million dollars in unrestricted support for the research I university. Again, this factor might logically be correlated to the political and cultural makeup of a state. States with historically high taxes, such as Wisconsin, come out of more progressive traditions than more fiscally conservative states like Ohio. The disposition of a state's culture also has important implications for the type of lawmakers that residents will elect.

Finally, it is important to briefly restate the limitations of both the quantitative and qualitative analyses in this study. First, the regression analysis was built with limits on the availability of data, preventing a full range of factors to be considered in the analysis. In addition, I used my own discretion to define the indicators representing the theoretical strands present in the conceptual framework. As for the qualitative phase of this study, conclusions were drawn from only three case studies and a limited number of interviewees from each site, thereby limiting the generalizablity of the findings. Within these limitations, however, the conclusions provide compelling pieces of evidence from which to build future studies.

IMPLICATIONS FOR POLICY AND STRATEGY

The findings from the study show that the issue of state-university partnerships is complex and impossible to fully address by implementing a prescribed set of tactics and strategies to garner greater state support. Instead, the approach to improving funding streams is multi-faceted, involving larger shifts in culture and philosophy. Evidence of this shift can be seen in new partnerships between organizations and individuals at a number of levels. While the complexity of these relationships is recognized, the following sections isolate three levels of partnerships most critical to the survival of research universities, offering avenues for building stronger state-governance-campus relations. The following strategies and policy considerations are advanced to provide discussion points for campus administrators, governing boards, and government officials as they plan for the future of higher education in their states.

RESEARCH UNIVERSITIES

Commitment to Public Service and Outreach

This study suggests that research universities must find new ways to update their public service outreach mission in order to earn greater support in the 21st Century. A deeper campus commitment to these efforts would help institutions, land-grant universities in particular, reclaim their image as the state problem solver. Evidence suggests that a shift in philosophy towards increased public service would garner greater gubernatorial, legislative, and public support for the institution, which would eventually be realized in the form of greater appropriations. Put simply, a stronger partnership with the state begins with a clear commitment to state needs.

One way to spur this necessary change is to reevaluate the current structure of outreach and public service at these universities. Placing the extension role firmly under the management of the research land-grant university (as opposed to an independent extension campus or among other regional campuses) seems critical to helping the institution define itself as the state's primary source for economic development. In order to be a useful resource to the general public and state officials, outreach at the campuses must be centralized to provide a recognizable clearinghouse of information about the public service activities of the campus. As evidenced by the review of UGA, a more formalized outreach structure seems critical to helping the research universities track, coordinate, and communicate the outreach activities of institution. Related to state appropriations, this structure is also an effective way to garner greater public support for the university.

But the commitment to public service must go beyond a change in structure. Rather, the programs and reward system of research universities must accurately reflect the commitment to serving the state. In other words, campus administrators and faculty governance must fully support and reward professors who pursue public service activities. Put simply, the mission of public service and outreach is hollow without a committed group of faculty and staff dedicated to achieving these goals. The University of Georgia's public service career ladder may provide one model for institutions to consider.

Focus on Accountability

Ultimately, campuses are viewed as accountable when the public understands and appreciates the work of the university, and how it is benefiting the state as a whole. In other words, government officials and the public at large demand to know how the university is using public resources to help the people of the state. At the same time, efficiency and the wise use of resources is also important. Faculty workload, time-to-degree and other accountability issues must continue to be addressed and clearly communicated to the legislature and public-at-large. Public support for research universities depends in large part on the institution's credibility as a good steward of state tax dollars.

HIGHER EDUCATION GOVERNANCE

Innovative Approaches to Economic Development

The findings of this study suggest that state higher education governing bodies can help research universities earn greater state support by focusing on building stronger partnerships between institutions and private industry for the purpose of developing state economy and assisting with social problems. Georgia's ICAPP program is a good example of an initiative that leverages the resources of all the state universities toward a particular outcome. Other states might follow the ICAPP example by conducting a needs assessment with business and community leaders to determine the most critical areas meriting attention. These needs could be linked to existing or new educational opportunities to achieve these goals. Collaborative efforts with the private sector are also an important component—soliciting the participation of a state's private universities. The research I university has the expertise, and arguably, the responsibility to take a leadership role in the development of these programs.

In addition, state higher education governance structures must work with the research I campus to develop more effective means to communicate its impact to the state. While research universities must take the brunt of the responsibility for communicating their contributions, the governance structure can support their efforts by confirming and legitimizing the institution's unique role among state campuses. This study pointed out that the University System of Georgia has clearly developed and communicated the complimentary roles among the public universities in that state. On the opposite end, the Ohio Board of Regents has struggled with creating and demonstrating complimentary work of Ohio campuses, and the unique role that Ohio State University plays as the state's land grant institution. These challenges are largely due to strong historical and cultural factors that inhibit OSU from claiming its status as the flagship institution. In any event, effective governance structures will demonstrate how each of the campuses provide a broader benefit to the state's economy and residents' quality of life. This approach must go beyond economic impact statements about jobs and revenue, rather, the focus on public service and economic development must become embedded into the institutional culture, and subsequently, the state culture.

STATE GOVERNMENT

Investment in Higher Education

This study suggests that governors and legislators have a enormous impact on the extent of state support for the research I university. The case studies revealed that gubernatorial and legislative support has revolutionized higher education in Georgia, whereas political influences in Ohio and Wisconsin has kept support for OSU and UW at modest levels in recent years.

Recent conservative approaches to funding higher education threaten the quality, access, and affordability of U.S. colleges and universities. Present trends continued, sacrifices to one or more of these goals will wittingly or unwittingly be made. Doing its part, a refocused, accountable research university and governance structure that better serves economic development goals would merit more support. The challenge for states is to provide the necessary resources to help governing boards and campuses achieve these objectives. With the help of campuses and governing boards, governors and legislators might rediscover the potential of research universities and be motivated to increase state investment in higher education.

History and Political Momentum

Most often, colleges and universities are the product of political history. As the study suggests, this was the case with Wisconsin's Robert LaFollette in the early part of this century and Georgia's Zell Miller in more recent years. In both examples, the groundswell in support for higher education came from strong political factions that placed colleges and universities in the forefront of the state agenda. LaFollette's progressive movement invested in higher education to advance the state economy, while Miller's HOPE scholarship is doing the same in the present era. As this study showed, Ohio has yet to elect a higher education governor and legislature that has had the same effect as Miller and LaFollette. Rather, Ohio is defined by the strength of its blue-collar community, which has continued to elect fiscally conservative governors and lawmakers.

The case study of Wisconsin further suggests the fragile nature of state culture and how political influences can cause significant cultural shifts in a relatively short period of time. Over a ten-year span, Wisconsin and its long-standing tradition of quality, access, and affordability has been threatened by a more conservative approach toward funding. This political sentiment emerged in response to high taxes in the state, whereas public colleges and universities became the targets of budget cuts. Due to this powerful shift in philosophy, the landscape of support for the UW System has changed significantly in the past decade.

These examples suggest that research universities are seemingly helpless to the outside forces that dictate levels of public support for colleges and universities. While the implication is that campuses are forced to be reactive, rather than proactive, institutions might act proactively by attempting to influence the state culture—creating conditions leading to the election of pro-higher education governors and legislators, for example. In particular, campuses that rally grassroots supporters who hold prominent positions have shown to have a positive effect on garnering state support. As chapter two discussed, the Virginia Higher Education Business Council was a grassroots effort comprised of high profile business leaders that helped to elect pro-higher education politicians in that state. Of the most important outcomes, the newly elected official brought about funding improvements for public colleges and universities in Virginia. This example speaks to the importance of state relations strategies and their implications for bringing about important political shifts.

ORGANIZATIONAL THEORY CONCLUSIONS

In chapter two, rational, political, and cultural systems theories were introduced as the theoretical bedrock of this study. Building on the current literature, the findings and conclusions of this study offer additional insights related to these three perspectives. In this section, the perspectives are reintroduced to build bridges and fill in gaps between theories that explain organizational processes and structures surrounding state support for research universities. Stated another way, the goal of the following analysis is to weave the existing theoretical constructs with the new findings and examine which of the combinations of theories are ultimately most compelling to explain variations in state support for research universities.

Rational Systems Theories: "Data Driven"

The rational systems perspective views organizations in terms of being mechanical and "data-driven." In this theoretical approach, organizations are viewed as machines designed to achieve predetermined goals and objectives, organized in a way that promotes optimal efficiency (Morgan, 1986). Related to state appropriations for colleges and universities, the rational perspective would suggest that states collect and analyze data to determine levels of resources needed to keep these "machines" working. Accordingly, it would assume that institutions themselves create rational structures and strategies aimed to garner maximum support for their operations. These ideas are tested through a closer look at the rational choice and competitive strategy theories as they relate to the conclusions advanced in this study.

Rational choice and bounded rationality theory:

Rational choice and bounded rationality suggest that optimal decisions are made based on an objective review of data and investigation of alternative choices (Cyert and March, 1963). As the fishbone diagram illustrates in figure 2.1, rational indicators are often organized around the economic health and demographic characteristics of the state. While the literature review asserts that legislators use rational measures, such as economic and demographic data, to make decisions about higher education budgeting, the findings from this study suggest that these factors play only a small role in explaining differences in state support for research I universities.

This conclusion is advanced for two reasons. First, the state wealth and demographic indicators were not shown to be significant in the regression analysis. In fact, only one rational indicator, per capita taxes, was included in the final model, suggesting that tax policies have some effect on higher education support. But as the next section argues, this factor is arguably more political than rational due to the nature of political alliances supporting higher or lower tax rates. Second, the case investigations of Ohio, Wisconsin and Georgia economies clearly illustrated the modest role that economic indicators play in predicting state support. For instance, Wisconsin, Ohio, and Georgia have all enjoyed healthy economies throughout the late 1990s, however, elected officials in each state have chosen to spend additional resources differently. When the economy struggled during the recession of the early 1990s, Ohio and Wisconsin made drastic cuts to higher education which were slow to rebound, whereas Georgia made only slight reductions and rebounded quickly. In these examples, the cases demonstrate that the strength of the economy does not necessarily lead to a boost in higher education funding, or conversely, that a weak economy forecasts a sharp decline investment in all colleges and universities.

Based on these findings, this study argues that an application of rational choice theory is only mildly relevant to understanding differences in higher education budgets and the extent to which policy makers support higher education.

Competitive strategy theory:

While the application of rational systems theory offers only a minor explanation of how state-level processes and structures explain differences in support for colleges and universities, an application of rational theories is more useful when it is viewed at the institutional level. In particular, there is clear evidence that competitive strategy is used by research universities to legitimize their activities and compete with other campuses and agencies seeking state dollars. In short, competitive strategy theory argues that organizational leaders choose optimum strategies to compete with other resource dependent entities given regulators, competitors, and barriers (Child, 1973). Furthermore, organizations are driven to incorporate the practices and procedures defined by prevailing rationalized concepts of organizational work that are institutionalized in society (Meyer and Rowan, 1977).

The case studies suggested that institutions, in developing strong state-university partnerships, create rational structures and activities to accomplish institutionalized goals and demonstrate their legitimacy among state decision-makers. As the study suggests, UGA has focused on its relationship with the state more so than OSU and UW, and has adopted a competitive strategy approach to legitimize its activities among state stakeholders. UGA's strategy has been to set up a centralized structure to efficiently and effectively attend to the public service needs of the state, operating strong, visible programs that are clearly committed to strengthening the state economy and improving Georgian's quality of life. The most obvious evidences of this strategy are seen in the formal operation of the Office of Outreach and Public Service, the unique public service faculty track program, and the participation with Georgia's Intellectual Capital Partnership Program (ICAPP).

But before broad praise can be given for UGA's state relations success compared to the other two institutions, one can not make the assumption that all three campuses are equally focused on this effort. Revisiting each campuses sources of funding makes this point. As the pie charts revealed, UGA's sources of funding come significantly more from state appropriations than both UW and OSU. Specifically, 45 percent of UGA's budget comes from state appropriations as compared to 24 percent at OSU and 23 percent at UW. Furthermore, the differences in the national scope and stature of the campuses is reflected in the differences in federal and private grants between the three institutions. Approximately 25 percent of UW-Madison's budget comes from federal grants and private contracts as opposed to 12 percent at UGA and 10 percent at OSU. Noting this observation, it might be argued that UW-Madison's competitive strategy is more concentrated on maintaining its national focus, and thus, the external relations strategies are more balanced between the federal and state government.

Finally, this argument might be extended to the differences in accountability between the three institutions. The cases showed that UGA is very focused on showing accountability to the state, whereas UW and OSU have been less focused on this area. Again, because of the differences in sources of funding, UW and OSU might concentrate more on federal and corporate accountability as opposed to state accountability like UGA.

Political Systems Theories: "Power Driven"

This study suggests that political theories are particularly relevant when they are used to understand differences in state support for research I universities. Both the regression analysis and case studies showed that individuals and political coalitions push and pull in the higher education policy environment and ultimately lead to the final budget outcome. Thus, higher education budgeting decisions using this perspective are likely to be seen as "power-driven." This study animated how power is significant at the macro level (politics at the state level), and the micro level (politics between institutions and higher education governance structures.) A review of strategic contingency, resource dependency, and coalition building theories demonstrate the important political struggles at these varying levels.

Strategic contingency theory:

Strategic contingency theory suggests that the course of an organization will be determined by power actors, or groups of power holders, that best manage uncertainty in an organization (Scott, 1992). Uncertainty can be defined as a lack of information about future events, so that alternatives and their outcomes are unpredictable. Actors that are most likely to best manage this uncertainty are those who are difficult to substitute and are central to many of the activities in the organization (Hickson, Hinings, Lee, Schneck, Pennings, 1977). Simply put, the theory suggests that organizations often depend on the influence of powerful actors who are critical to determining an institution's fate.

On the state level, the power of the governor emerged as the strategic contingency that most determined the fate of the institutions in the case studies, reinforcing the literature suggesting that governors may have the strongest political impact on support for higher education. In Georgia, Governor Zell Miller was the key power that placed higher education as the top priority in the state, while the governors in Wisconsin and Ohio used their power to support competing initiatives. In each case, gubernatorial influence set the tone for the legislative response to funding higher education.

Resource dependency theory:

As chapter two pointed out, the central premise of resource dependency is that an organization needs to extract resources from the environment to survive and in effect, place other competing organizations into external dependencies. Organizations, therefore, pursue political strategies that will enhance their bargaining position among other dependent agencies. How important and how scarce these resources are determines the nature and the extent of dependency (Pfeffer and Salancik, 1978).

In this study, the impact of resource dependency was shown to be relevant on two different planes. First, the emergence of "new" federalism as described in chapter two has seemingly magnified the power struggle between competing state agencies; particularly between higher education, K-12 schools, corrections, and health care. However, as this study pointed out, the struggle that faces higher education seems to be less of a squeeze due to direct competition with state agencies, but rather a product of differing priorities by powerful elected leaders. This especially appears to be true because the strong economy of the late 1990s resulted in a surplus of tax dollars in most states, and thus competition for scarce resources became less important. Instead, an agency's justification for needing the additional revenues became the determining factor. Thus, resource dependency may be a useful way to explain variations in higher education funding to the extent that state agencies have access and the ability to shape the positions of state lawmakers.

Beyond this observation, the resource dependency perspective might be best applied to the way one thinks about differences in higher education governance. In Ohio, it became clear that the weak coordinating board structure has allowed powerful regional campuses to place other campuses into competing dependencies. While history also was shown to play an important role in these struggles, the board has not been effective in mitigating these problems. On the other hand, this study suggests that stronger governance systems, such as the UW System and University System of Georgia, may be more effective in preventing competitive struggles than coordinating boards. The implication is that competition for resources may vary in intensity between campuses depending on the strength of the higher education governance structure in a particular state. Put differently, the strength of resource dependence as an explanatory theory might depend on the relative strength of the state's governance structure.

Coalition building:

Coalitions are subsets of individuals and groups that share consensual goals and work toward a common end (Cyert and March, 1963). Often, organizations form coalitions for the purpose of accruing mutual benefits (Scott, 1992). The literature review in chapter two underscored the importance of coalitions as a way to leverage support for colleges and universities. In particular, the business and higher education community in Virginia mutually benefited when they rallied support for higher education to bring about economic growth in the state.

In this study, the strength of coalition arrangements became evident in a review of Georgia's higher education system. Georgia's Intellectual Capital Partnership Program has leveraged the vast resources of the state's 34 public colleges and universities on behalf of economic development, and has subsequently increased state dollars for the campuses. The partnership between the campuses and private industry has garnered additional dollars into the University System of Georgia in exchange for the promise to attract high-quality, high-growth knowledge-based industries.

Along the same lines, the Georgia Research Alliance represents a coalition between Georgia's public and private research universities and corporate partners. The purpose of the Alliance is to escalate the research capabilities of Georgia's research universities as a way to improve Georgia's economic future. Again, a positive consequence of the research coalition is that it has leveraged significant state dollars that are then distributed to the participating units.

Both types of coalitions could be regarded as a distributive coalition, because the primary focus is on influencing the distribution of resources to organizational members (Scott, 1992). In the ICAPP and Georgia Research Alliance programs, additional state dollars benefit all the participating campuses. Looking at these examples, coalition-building theory merits consideration as it is used to understand how collaborative arrangements can leverage state dollars in support for research universities.

Culture "Values and Symbols Driven"

Morgan (1986) notes that cultural symbols and rituals, attitudes, opinion, and general conditions shape organizational reality. The findings from this study supports Layzell and Lyddon's (1990) assertion that state culture has an important impact on the extent to which institutions are supported by their states. In keeping with this cultural paradigm, higher education budgeting decisions might be labeled as "values/symbols driven." In the following sections, the four cultural theories outlined in the conceptual framework will be reintroduced to understand their relevance in explaining differences in state appropriations for research universities.

Obligatory action and enactment theory

Obligatory action suggests that behavior can be viewed as contractual implicit agreements to act appropriately in return for being treated appropriately (March, 1981). Instead of contemplating alternatives, values and consequences, the decision-maker asks, "what kind of situation is this?" "what kind of person am I?" and "what is appropriate for me to do in a situation like this?" (March, 1981). Similarly, enactment theory suggests that decisions are driven by assumptions of "how things need to be" or by general perceptions of what is happening. In essence, the model theorizes that values and goals are manipulated or shaped organizationally and are then ultimately expressed as givens. In this case, a paradigm is developed over time and eventually embedded within the general belief systems of decision-makers or the public at large (Suchman, 1996).

Reviewing the case studies, it became clear that obligatory action and enactment theory have an important explanatory role in understanding the differences in state support for research universities. As for obligatory action, comments by the legislators and campuses legitimized the notion that attitudes and perceptions about "what's appropriate" influences higher education budgets. For example, UW-Madison's decline in funding might be traced to the fact that many legislators view the institution as "ungrateful, out-of-touch, and unable to demonstrate their worth." Similarly, Ohio State Universities funding plight might be explained for comparable reasons. As one interviewee put it, "OSU is not there offering to help... they are in the ivory tower doing research, but not helping down the street." On the other hand, Georgia lawmakers are seemingly compelled to support the institution because of the obvious benefits it provides to state citizens. As one legislator explained, "UGA is seen as having people out in the community in response to them. The fact is that citizens feel that their lives have been enriched because of the outreach program."

Tied to obligatory action theory, these findings suggest that legislators will uphold the implicit agreement to act appropriately (providing adequate funding) in return for being treated appropriately (campuses attending to the needs of the state). In Ohio and Wisconsin, legislators did not feel that they and their constituents were being treated appropriately, and thus they are not heavily supporting these institutions. In Georgia, legislators saw the positive effects of UGA outreach and are thus more inclined to support the institution.

Enactment theory would suggest that, over time, a paradigm is developed and becomes embedded within the general belief systems of decision-makers or the public at large. This may be most evident in Ohio, as OSU continues to struggle financially due to the historically conservative approach to funding. The strong blue-collar mentality has become embedded in Ohio's culture, making it more difficult to turn the attention to higher education. Using this logic, UW-Madison should remain a highly supported campus because of its historical pattern of high support. But as the study showed, political shifts and institutional drift from the land-grant mission may be responsible for the more moderate support that exists today.

As for the University of Georgia, obligatory action and enactment theory seem less useful for explaining the high level of support that it enjoys today. Instead, another cultural theory—symbolic decision-making—seems to provide a compelling explanation for UGA's boost in support throughout the 1990s.

Symbolic decision-making theory:

Symbolic decision-making theory suggests that a powerful actor reinforces or promotes a value through specific actions, and complementing language and symbols supporting that particular action and value. Schein (1992) speaks of these actions as ways that "cultural managers" can effectively influence organizations. Cultural managers externalize their own assumptions and embed them consistently in organizational missions and goals (Schein, 1992).

The most clear example of symbolic decision-making in this study can be seen in the actions of former Georgia Governor Zell Miller. Miller used his power to promote the values of higher education, reinforcing his beliefs through the creation of the HOPE scholarship program and increases in faculty salaries. These initiatives stand as tangible symbols of Miller's commitment to shifting the state culture to focus more intently on higher education. Miller is a prime example of a cultural manager that used his political influence to cause a groundswell of cultural change in the state. His investment in higher education stands as a mark of his commitment to raise the historically weak academic standards in order that Georgia might become a cultural and economic leader of the South.

Institutional theory:

Institutional theorists contend that organizational structures and messages can serve as an important signaling mechanism to the organization's constituencies about the values of an organization. Institutional theory emphasizes that organizations are open systems that are strongly influenced by their environments—but that many of these forces are not the result of rational pressures for more effective performance, but of social and cultural pressures to conform to conventional beliefs (Scott, 1992). Meyer and Rowan (1977) argue that formal structures of organizations have meaning and importance regardless of whether they affect the behaviors of performers in the technical core, but that they effectively symbolize meaning and order.

In this study, institutional theory might be best understood by reviewing the difference in structures and marketing strategies aimed to promote the public service activities of the case study institutions. Institutional theorists would argue, for example, that the University of Georgia has been successful in demonstrating their service to the state, simply because they have formal structures and strategies in place to convey the importance of public service. As was outlined in the study, these structures and strategies include the formal Office of Public Service and Outreach, the public service career track, and the exclusive marketing efforts aimed to promote the institution among a variety of constituents. On the other hand, the public service structures and strategies established by UW and OSU are arguably absent from the view of legislators and the public at large, explaining the financial struggles at the institutions. The fact is that UW and OSU's decentralized approach to public service, combined with the campuses limited effort in promoting a cohesive message about the impact of public service, does little to symbolize institutional commitment to outreach.

While these structures and strategies are important, institutional theory takes it a step further, arguing that the visibility of the structures and strategies are actually more critical than the outcomes they aim to accomplish. In other words, formal public service structures and marketing strategies themselves sufficiently symbolize meaning in order, regardless if they are actually effective in improving service to the state. To that end, this study argues that institutional theory has a limited role in explaining the differences in state appropriations for research universities. Instead, the findings suggest that institutions must clearly demonstrate their success in this area rather than simply relying on symbols or structures to send the message that public service is important.

The OSU story about the "tenure-denied" faculty member makes this point. As the case study revealed, state officials were outraged when a prominent faculty member was denied tenure despite his outstanding contributions to state educational policy. During this tribulation, the campus president and university relations officers continued to send legislators the messages about the importance of outreach on the OSU campus. The problem was that the actions of the tenure committee revealed an inconsistency between the symbols being relayed by campus officials and the actual outcomes surrounding a commitment to public service. Said one member of the legislature, "This incident clearly sent the message to the State that public service is not valued by OSU. We hear the message of public service in speeches but don't see it in practice." It is clear that this well publicized contradiction damaged former President Gordon Gee's credibility in promoting the value of OSU to the State. Declared one state official, "The President (Gee) can talk all he wants, but it's just not happening."

Based on this evidence, this study argues that competitive strategy theory may make a more compelling theoretical model than institutional theory. Competitive strategy suggests that institutions must construct rational structures and strategies to legitimately pursue and benchmark public service goals, rather than relying on symbols to make the case that these activities are important. Put in the simplest terms, this study suggests that campuses actually have to "do something" rather than just saying that they are "doing something"—clearly demonstrating their benefit rather than just producing symbols to suggest its benefit.

Intersection of Factors and Theory

The previous analyses presented factors and theoretical constructs in the study most useful for understanding differences in state support for research universities. While these individual factors and perspectives are important on their own, it is important to note that it is the combination of these factors and constructs that provide the complete picture of state support for these types of institutions. In other words, it is the totality and multiple combinations of these compelling factors and theoretical perspectives that explain underlying differences in institutional support.

Figure 8.1 illustrates the synergy that these factors and perspectives present, creating bridges between political, cultural, and structural factors to explain their effect on various organizational levels: state, higher education governance, and institutional.

Figure 8.1 outlines a few of the vast combinations of factors and theories that work together to explain differences in support for research universities. To illustrate their interaction, the following paragraphs present selected examples of the flow between each point on the triangle. First, the bridge between the political and cultural perspectives is critically important to fully understanding state appropriations for research universities. The governor especially intersects both perspectives. As the analysis of strategic contingency suggested, the governor is a powerful actor that has supreme political influence over the investment in higher education spending. However, governors may be driven more by cultural factors rather than political ones. Governors may be influenced to support higher education based on whether they feel that campuses have earned the right to be well supported, thereby, supporting the obligatory action theory. Furthermore, the studies showed that governors are often symbolic in their decision-making, proposing budgets to either reinforce the value of higher education or to make a statement about making an important change.

Just as important, the existing culture of the state significantly affects whether or not a progressive governor with a strong disposition to support higher education will actually be elected. That is, the historic traditions often determine the dominant political agenda of the state. As the case study of OSU revealed, the State of Ohio has long been dominated by a fiscally conservative culture, still evident by the current body of elected officials representing conservative values.

The structural and political points on the triangle also illustrate the crossover of complementary theoretical constructs and factors. One example can be seen in the interpretation of resource dependency as it relates to the strength and structure of higher education governing bodies in a state. As the study showed, the type of governance structure can predict the extent to which power and dependence between campuses play a role in determining support for institutions. In other words, the type of structure itself may drive whether politics is an important factor in budgeting decisions. On the other hand, state politics have a heavy role in determining the type of higher education governance structure in place. Political forces are at work in determining the governance arrangement between public universities, often influenced by the strength of governors and local district legislators that vie for optimal support for their particular campuses.

But higher education governance example is also useful to examine the flow between the structural and cultural points of the triangle. One could argue that the type of higher education governance is actually the product of the state culture, which in turn drives the political process. Again, the case studies illustrate

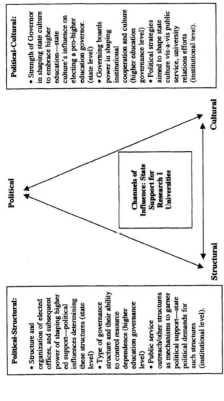
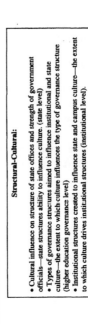

Political-Cultural:
- Strength of Governor in shaping state culture to embrace higher education—state culture's influence on electing a pro-higher education governor. (state level)
- Governing boards power in shaping institutional cooperation and culture (higher education governance level)
- Political strategies aimed to shape state culture vis-a-vis public service, university relations efforts (institutional level).

Political

Cultural

Channels of Influence: State Support for Research I Universities

Structural

Political-Structural:
- Structure and organization of elected offices, and subsequent power of shaping higher ed support—political influences determining these structures (state level)
- Type of governance structure and their ability to control resource dependence (higher education governance level)
- Public service outreach/other structures as mechanisms to garner political support—state political demands for such structures (institutional level).

Structural-Cultural:
- Cultural influence on structure of state offices and strength of government officials—state structures ability to influence culture. (state level)
- Types of governance structures aimed to influence institutional and state culture—the extent to which culture influences the type of governance structure (higher education governance level)
- Institutional structures created to influence state and campus culture—the extent to which culture drives institutional structures (institutional level).

Figure 8.1 A Model of State Support for Public Research I Universities

this point. Ohio has strong regional cultures or "city states" comprised of citizens that have strong allegiance to their regional universities—areas like Toledo, Cincinnati, and Akron. It could be argued that the regional cultures are so strong that they are the determining forces that resist the consolidation of the state universities into a united system. As the case studies of UGA and UW suggested, these regional affiliations are not as strong in Georgia and Wisconsin, which might explain the ability for a consolidated system of higher education to form in these states. This particular example illustrates the interplay between each of the points of the triangle, as the governance factor can easily be viewed through multiple lenses.

Finally, the model shows the complex and complementary relationships that exist between all factors at all organizational levels. The importance of these relationships merit more investigation, which will be explored more completely in the last section outlining opportunities for future research.

SIGNIFICANCE OF THE STUDY

As the introduction in chapter one pointed out, the study of state appropriations for higher education is important because it addresses the critical issue of institutional survival. Because state appropriations continue to be among the most important sources of higher education funding, continued research surrounding this critical revenue source remains fundamental. The fact that colleges and universities rely on state support to remain viable and healthy is the most obvious reason for the emphasis on this topic.

The results of this study are especially valuable to research university leaders because it suggests ways to enhance their institution's positions within their states. This comparative study of state appropriations places empirical evidence behind the assertion that future state support for research universities will be contingent on an institution's ability to demonstrate its service to the state. This study further animated the importance of two partners critical to regaining support: higher education governing boards and state governments. First, governing boards play an important role in defining the objectives of campuses, monitoring the accountability of these institutions, and demonstrating innovation related to economic development. Second, the partnership between the governor and the legislature is the key to ensuring the future of higher education, and subsequently, the future economic health of the state. In sum, the study clearly pointed out the necessary partnership to achieve multiple goals in state public higher education.

Finally, this research is significant because it provides a service to a broad range of state and university constituencies as they collectively wrestle with planning for the financial future of higher education. Besides providing a general framework by which to understand the arena of important issues and factors, the findings ultimately inform university administrators about what it takes to earn the support of the state, and state officials about the benefits of increased investment in higher education.

In addition to practitioners and lawmakers, the study is useful to higher education scholars because it strengthens the higher education politics and finance literature—filling in important gaps about systems, processes, and structures associated with strong state support for research institutions. For organizational theorists, the new conceptual framework builds bridges between current perspectives and theories related to the organization and governance of higher education. While the framework needs further testing, the study has made important strides towards explaining organizational reasons behind the variation in state support for research I universities over the past ten years.

IMPLICATIONS FOR FUTURE RESEARCH

The findings from this study offer a wealth of opportunities for further research focused on state support for research universities. The study itself could be strengthened by expanding the methods and approaches used to derive the findings advanced in this analysis. On the qualitative side, additional case studies could be undertaken to build on what was learned in three studies investigated. Expanding the number of case sites and institutions would strengthen the generalizability of the study, and may provide additional clues not captured in the study of OSU, UW, and UGA.

As for the quantitative analysis, alternative definitions might be used in a new regression analysis to expand the landscape of indicators that might define state support beyond unrestricted state appropriations. Testing alternative definitions of state support under the same model would accommodate for other complex indicators that can not be factored in using one indicator alone. For example, some institutional leaders point to the importance of tuition flexibility as being included in the overall package of support that a state provides. The argument is that autonomy and freedom are important factors that are less measurable in state taxes, but allow for the availability of support from other sources. In a future study, the dependant variable might include state appropriations combined with tuition and fees revenue as a way to capture this flexibility. Using this model, the balance of the study could be replicated using the methods presented in this dissertation.

Beyond these approaches to strengthening this study, future research should build on the factors that emerged as most important in this analysis. A stronger lens should be used to take a more in-depth look at each of these factors and how they contribute to an understanding of state support for research universities. In particular, the role of governors, public service operations, and governance structures merit further research as they have been linked to having an important impact on institutional survival. Furthermore, the interactions of each of these factors paired with various organizational levels should be studied as a way to examine the relative importance of these partnerships. The strength of this approach is that it broadens the focus beyond institutional reform to recognize the importance of other key partners in the process. Table 8:1 provides a matrix of possible research questions that intersect the key factors identified in this study with various organizational levels that influence state support.

Table 8.1 Matrix of Future Research Opportunities

Key support factors identified in study	Levels of Influence		
	State level	*Higher Education Governance level*	*Institutional level*
Gubernatorial influences	How does the relationship between governors, legislators, and state agencies affect the level of state support for research universities?	To what extent does the partnership between governors and higher education governance leaders impact state support for research universities?	What factors promote strong institutional-gubernatorial relationships?
Public Service and Outreach	What are examples of state leaders, agencies, and the greater public that recognize the public service benefits of research universities? What mechanisms are in place that best facilitate this visibility?	What role should higher education governing boards have in supporting public service efforts among research universities? What model is most efficient and effective toward achieving public service goals?	What are the best practices of outreach units as they related to demonstrating institutional service to the state? To what extent does this affect state support?
Strength of Higher Education Governance	What are examples of strong partnerships between higher education governance structures and states? To what extent does this impact state support for research institutions?	What are the best practices of governing boards as they relate to improving state support for research universities?	What are examples of strong partnerships between research I universities and higher education governance structures? What impact does this have on state support for the institution?

Finally, this study provides additional research opportunities in the realm of organizational theory. Because the analysis has identified preliminary linkages between the rational, political, and cultural perspectives, the accompanying theories merit more investigation, as they are useful to explain the internal and external processes, structures, and events corresponding to differences in state support for research universities. One example of further investigation related to the cultural perspective, is to more closely review the influence of governors and the role they play in managing and developing state culture. As this study suggests, governors are important cultural managers that, through policy, can cause significant shifts in the way that citizens view higher education. A historical account comparing governors such as Robert LaFollette and Zell Miller would animate the importance of these leaders and the critical influences they had on shaping a state citizen's view of higher education.

In closing, this study represents a small step towards addressing the great landscape of fiscal issues confronting higher education administrators and scholars today. As the preceding discussion made clear, there is much more to learn and contribute. Through further research, it is hoped that a strong framework can be developed to help all interested stakeholders as they work together to ensure the vitality of public research universities in the 21st Century.

CARNEGIE PUBLIC RESEARCH I UNIVERSITIES

Source: The Carnegie Foundation for the Advancement of Teaching. A Classification of Institutions of Higher Education (1994). Foreword by Ernest Boyer, San Francisco: Jossey-Bass, Inc. Publisher

ALABAMA

University of Alabama at Birmingham

ARIZONA

Arizona State University
University of Arizona

CALIFORNIA

University of California at Berkeley
University of California at Davis
University of California at Irvine
University of California at Los Angeles
University of California at San Diego
University of California at San Francisco
University of California at Santa Barbara

COLORADO

Colorado State University
University of Colorado at Boulder

CONNECTICUT

University of Connecticut

FLORIDA

Florida State University
University of Florida

GEORGIA

Georgia Institute of Technology
University of Georgia

HAWAII

University of Hawaii at Manoa

ILLINOIS

University of Illinois at Chicago
University of Illinois at Urbana—at Champaign

INDIANA

Indiana University at Bloomington
Purdue University, Main Campus

IOWA

Iowa State University
University of Iowa

KANSAS

University of Kansas, Main Campus

KENTUCKY

University of Kentucky

LOUISIANA

Louisiana State University and Agricultural and Mechanical College

MARYLAND

University of Maryland at College Park

MASSACHUSETTS

University of Massachusetts at Amherst

MICHIGAN

Michigan State University
University of Michigan at Ann Arbor
Wayne State University

MINNESOTA

University of Minnesota at Twin Cities

MISSOURI

University of Missouri at Columbia

NEBRASKA

University of Nebraska at Lincoln

NEW JERSEY

Rutgers the State University of New Jersey, New Brunswick Campus

NEW MEXICO

New Mexico State University, Main Campus
University of New Mexico, Main Campus

NEW YORK

State University of New York at Buffalo
State University of New York at Stony Brook

NORTH CAROLINA

North Carolina State University
University of North Carolina at Chapel Hill

OHIO

Ohio State University, Main Campus
The University of Cincinnati, Main Campus

OREGON

Oregon State University

PENNSYLVANIA

Pennsylvania State University, Main Campus
Temple University
University of Pittsburgh, Pittsburgh Campus

TENNESSEE

University of Tennessee at Knoxville

TEXAS

Texas A & M University
University of Texas at Austin

UTAH

University of Utah
Utah State University

VIRGINIA

University of Virginia
Virginia Commonwealth University
Virginia Polytechnic Institute and State University

WASHINGTON

University of Washington

WEST VIRGINIA

West Virginia University

WISCONSIN

University of Wisconsin at Madison

Multiple Regression Variables, Metric, and Data Sources

Variable	Metric	Data Source
Dependant Variable		
Unrestricted state appropriations	Dollars	National Center for Educational Statistics, Integrated Postsecondary Education Data System (IPEDS). Finance and enrollment data files used for FY 1991-92 and FY 1996-97 http://nces.ed.gov/ipeds/data.html
Independent Variables		
Total state population	Total number	U.S. Census Bureau, United States Department of Commerce. Website: http://www.census.gov/
Population of college age residents (18-24)	Total number	U.S. Census Bureau, United States Department of Commerce. Website: http://www.census.gov/

Variable	Metric	Data Source
Dependant Variable		
Per capita income	Dollars	Bureau of Economic Analysis: United States Department of Commerce. Website: http://www.bea.doc.gov/
Per capita taxes	Dollars	U.S. Census Bureau, United States Department of Commerce. Website: http://www.census.gov/
Employment rate	Dollars	Federal Interagency Council on Statistical Policy (FEDSTATS) Website: http://www.fedstats.gov/
Party majority (republican or democrat) lower house during budget creation	Dummy variable: 1 signifies a republican majority, 0 signifies a democratic majority.	1991-1992 data: Vital statistics on American politics (1996). Washington, D.C.CQ Press. 1996-97 data: Project Vote Smart. Website: http://www.vote-smart.org/

Variable	Metric	Data Source
Dependant Variable		
Party majority (republican or democrat) upper house during budget creation	Dummy variable: 1 signifies a republican majority, 0 signifies a democratic majority.	1991-1992 data: Vital statistics on American politics (1996). Washington, D.C.CQ Press. 1996-97 data: Project Vote Smart. Website: http://www.vote-smart.org/
Republican or democratic governor during budget creation	Dummy variable: 1 signifies a republican governor, 0 signifies a democratic governor.	1991-1992 data: Vital statistics on American politics (1996). Washington, D.C.CQ Press. 1996-97 data: Project Vote Smart. Website: http://www.vote-smart.org/
Per capita spent on health care	Dollars	U.S. Census Bureau, United States Department of Commerce. Website: http://www.census.gov/
Per capita spent on corrections	Dollars	U.S. Census Bureau, United States Department of Commerce. Website: http://www.census.gov/

Variable	Metric	Data Source
Dependant Variable		
Per capita spent on education	Dollars	U.S. Census Bureau, United States Department of Commerce. Website: http://www.census.gov/
Consolidated governing board governing all state higher education institutions	Dummy variable: 1 indicates that the institution is governed under this arrangement, 0 signifies that it is not.	All governance structure data taken from: State Postsecondary Education Structures Sourcebook: State Coordinating and Governing Boards. Education Commission of the States: Denver, Colorado. (Volumes 1994 & 1997)
Coordinating board: regulatory power	Dummy variable: 1 indicates that the institution is governed under this arrangement, 0 signifies that it is not.	(see governance structure source above)
Coordinating board: advisory power	Dummy variable: 1 indicates that the institution is governed under this arrangement, 0 signifies that it is not.	(see governance structure source above)
Planning and service agency	Dummy variable: 1 indicates that the institution is governed under this arrangement, 0 signifies that it is not.	(see governance structure source above)

Variable	Metric	Data Source
Dependant Variable		
Number of public 4-year institutions in the state	Number of institutions	Digest of Education Statistics. U.S. Dept. of Health, Education, and Welfare, Education Division, National Center for Education Statistics: Washington, D.C. (Volumes 1992 & 1997).
Number of private 4-year institutions in the state	Number of institutions	Digest of Education Statistics. U.S. Dept. of Health, Education, and Welfare, Education Division, National Center for Education Statistics: Washington, D.C. (Volumes 1992 & 1997).
Total enrollment: full time undergraduate students	Numbers of students	All institutional characteristic data taken from the National Center for Educational Statistics, Integrated Postsecondary Education Data System (IPEDS). Finance and enrollment data files used for FY 1991-92 and FY 1996-97 http://nces.ed.gov/ipeds/data.html

Variable	Metric	Data Source
Dependant Variable		
Total enrollment: full time graduate students	Numbers of students	(see institutional characteristic source above)
Total tuition and fees revenue	Dollars	(see institutional characteristic source above)
Total private gifts and contracts	Dollars	(see institutional characteristic source above)
Total federal grants and contracts	Dollars	(see institutional characteristic source above)
Expenditures on instruction	Dollars	(see institutional characteristic source above)
Expenditures on research	Dollars	(see institutional characteristic source above)
Expenditures on public service	Dollars	(see institutional characteristic source above)

Interview Protocol

"Tell me about the factors that you believe best explain the level of state support for Institution X."

"From your perspective, what is happening in the State or on campus that best tells the story about the level of state support for Institution X."

TOPICAL AREAS

Economic and Demographic factors:

To what extent is funding for higher education in your state based on economic measures such as state tax capacity, availability of state revenues, and general economic conditions?

To what extent is funding for higher education and subsequently Institution X, based on changes in the overall population of the state, enrollment levels, and participation rates of the particular institutions?

Political factors:

Describe the politics of the budgeting process within your state, and explain how it affects appropriations for higher education, and Institution X, in particular.

To what extent does the Governor affect the level of appropriations for Institution X, and higher education in general? Historically, how important has the Governor been in planning for the future of higher education in your state?

Describe the political climate surrounding legislative support for Institution X. To what extent has this climate, or the actions of individual legislators, influenced the level of appropriations during the past decade?

What priority is given to higher education in your state, in particular Institution X, compared to other competing state agencies or programs such as corrections, K–12 schools, etc?

Higher Education Governance:

Describe the relationship between Institution X and the system or board that governs it.
How does the governance structure of higher education in your state affect the level of appropriations allocated to Institution X?

Within this governance structure, how does the method in which higher education funds are allocated influence the level of appropriations for Institution X?

Cultural Factors: (historical traditions/public attitudes)

Historically, to what degree has the state supported Institution X and higher education?

Describe the current level of citizens' collective value accorded to Institution X. What significant events or historical precedents may have shaped citizen's attitudes toward this institution?

To what degree do public attitudes reflect the growth of appropriations for Institution X?

Historically, how has the legislature treated Institution X? What degree of autonomy or flexibility (e.g. tuition) has been afforded to Institution X since its existence?

Institutional Strategies and Characteristics:

Have institutional strategies been employed to maintain or strengthen state support for Institution X? Explain the reasons behind the success or failure of these strategies.

What characteristics does Institution X posses that may lend it more state support than other state campuses?

Bibliography

Berry, Richard. *The Wisconsin Idea . . . Then and Now*. Madison, WI: R. Berry, 1972.

Bogdan, Robert C. and Sari Knopp Bicklen. *Qualitative research for education: An introduction to theory and methods*. Needham Heights, MA: Simon & Schuster, 1992.

Borg, Walter R. and Meredith Damien Gall. *Educational Research: An Introduction*. New York: Pittman Publishing, 1989.

Blumenstyk, Goldie. "Demographics Study Center to Aid Higher-Education Policymakers," *The Chronicle of Higher Education*, Vol. 34, No. 43, A16 (1988).

Breaking the Social Contract: The Fiscal Crisis in Higher Education. New York: Commission on National Investment in Higher Education, Council for Aid to Education, An Independent Subsidiary of RAND, 1997.

Burke Joseph C. and Andreea M. Serban. "The Impact of State Budget Reductions in the 1990s: A View of Public Higher Education in Six States". Presentation to the Society for College and University Planning 33rd Annual Conference, Vancouver, Canada, 1998.

Burke Joseph C. and Andreea M. Serban. "Performance Funding: Fashionable or Emerging Trend?" *Community College Journal*. Vol. 68, No. 3, 27–29 (1997).

Child, John. "Organization, Structure, Environment, and Performance: The Role of Strategic Choice," *Sociology*. Vol. 1 No. 6, 1–17 (1973).

A Classification of Institutions of Higher Education. Foreword by Ernest L. Boyer. Palo Alto, CA: Carnegie Foundation for the Advancement of Education, 1994.

Conrad, Clifton F., Jennifer Grant Howarth and Susan Bolyard Millar. *A Silent Success: Master's Education in the United States*. Baltimore, MD: Johns Hopkins Press, 1993.

Cryer, Jonathan D. and Robert B. Miller. *Statistics for Business: Data Analysis and Modeling*. Boston, MA: PWS-Kent Publishing Company, 1991.

Cyert, Richard M.., and James G. March. *A Behavioral Theory of the Firm*. Englewood Cliffs, New Jersey: Prentice-Hall, Inc., 1963.

Eisner, Elliot. "On the differences between scientific and artistic approaches to qualitative research." *Educational Researcher,* Vol. 10, No. 4: 5–9, (1981).

Encyclopedia Americana, 1995. S.V. "Georgia."

Ewell, Peter. "Accountability and the Future of Self-Regulation." *Change.* Vol. 1, No. 26, 25–29 (1994).

Fenske, Robert H. and Jacob O. Stampen. Review of the book, High Performance Colleges: The Malcolm Baldridge Award as a Framework for Improving Higher Education. *Journal of College Student Development.* Vol. 38, No. 4, 432–434 (1997).

Firestone, William A. "Meaning in method: The rhetoric of quantitative and qualitative research." *Educational Researcher* Vol. 16, No. 7: 16–21 (1987).

Glesne, Corrine, and Alan Peshkin. *Becoming Qualitative Researchers: An Introduction.* White Plains, NY: Longman Publishers, 1992.

Gold, S. D. "The Outlook for State Support of Higher Education." In, *Financial Planning Under Economic Uncertainty.* edited by R. E. Anderson and J. W. Meyerson, San Francisco: Jossey-Bass Publishers, 1990.

Greene, Jennifer C., Valerie J. Caracelli and Wendy F. Graham. "Toward a conceptual framework for mixed-method evaluation designs." *Educational Evaluation and Policy Analysis,* Vol. 11, Fall: 255–274 (1989).

Grapevine: A Database of Tax Support for Higher Education. edited by E. Hines, Normal, IL: Illinois State University.

Guba, Egon G. "Toward a methodology of naturalistic inquiry in educational evaluation." Los Angeles, CA: University of California Press, 1978.

Hines, Edward R., *State Higher Education Appropriations.* Denver, CO: State Higher Education Executive Office, 1998.

Hines, Edward R. *Higher Education and State Governments: Renewed Partnership, Cooperation, or Competition?* ASHE-ERIC Higher Education Report No. 5. Association for the Study of Higher Education: Washington, D.C., 1998.

Hickson, D. J., C. A. Hinings, R. E. Lee, R.E., Schneck, and J. M. Pennings. "A Strategic Contingencies Theory of Organizational Power." *Administrative Sciences Quarterly,* Vol. 5, No. 3: 216–227 (1977).

Hines, Edward R., Hickrod, G. Alan, Pruyne, G.B, *State Support of Higher Education: From Expansion to Steady State to Decline, 1969–1989.* MacArthur/Spencer Series No. 9. Normal, Ill.: Center for Education Finance and Higher Education, 1989.

Howe, Kenneth, R. "Against the quantitative-qualitative incompatibility thesis, or dogmas die hard." *Educational Researcher* Vol. 17, No. 8, 10–16, (1988).

Integrated Postsecondary Education Data System (IPEDS). National Center for Educational Statistics, Finance data files and survey used for FY 1991–92 and FY 1996–97, *http://nces.ed.gov/ipeds/data.html*

Jick, Todd D. "Mixing Qualitative and Quantitative Methods: Triangulation in Action." In *Qualitative Methodology*, edited by J. Van Maanen, Beverly Hills, CA: Sage Publications, 1983.

Johnson, L.G. (1984). The Higher-Technology Connection: Academic/Industrial Cooperation for Economic Growth. ASHE-ERIC Higher Education Research Report No. 6. Washington, D.C: Association for the Study of Higher Education. ED 255 130. 129 pp MF-01.

Keane, M. J., and Daniel F. Ritsche. *Wisconsin at 150 Years.* State of Wisconsin: Legislative Reference Bureau, 1998

Kettl, Donald F., *Reinventing the Wisconsin Idea.* Madison, WI: Robert M. LaFollette School of Public Affairs, University of Wisconsin-Madison.

Krome, Margaret. "Dust off the Wisconsin Idea." *The Madison Capital Times*, 17 June 1999, sec. C10.

Layzell, Daniel T. and Jan W. Lyddon. *Budgeting for Higher Education at the State Level: Enigma, Paradox, and Ritual.* Washington, DC: ASHE-ERIC Higher Education Reports, 1990.

MacTaggart, Terrance J., *Restructuring Higher Education.* San Francisco, CA: Jossey-Bass Publishers, 1996.

Magrath, C. Peter. Statement on the Kellogg Commission on the Future of State and Land-Grant Universities. Washington, D.C. 30 January 1996.

Marshall Catherine, Douglas Mitchell, and Frederick Wirt. *Culture and Educational Policy in the American States.* New York: Falmer Press, 1989.

March, James G., "Decisions in Organizations and Theories of Choice," In *Perspectives on Organization Design and Behavior*, edited by A. Van de Ven and W. Joyce. New York: Wiley, 1981.

McGuinness, Aims C., "The Functions and Evolution of State Coordination and Governance in Postsecondary Education." In *1997 State Postsecondary Education Structures Sourcebook*. Denver, CO: Education Commission of the States, 1997.

McKeown, Mary P. and Daniel T. Layzell. "State Funding Formulas for Higher Education: Trends and Issues." *Journal of Education Finance.* Vol. 19, No. 2, 319–346, (1994).

Meyer, John W and Brian Rowan. "Institutionalized Organizations: Formal Structure as Mythy and Ceremony." *American Journal of Sociology*, Vol. 83, No. 2, 340–363. (1977).

Morgan, Gareth. *Images of Organization.* London: Sage Publications, 1986.

Mortenson, Thomas. "Postsecondary Education Opportunity." Mortenson Research Seminar on Public Policy Analysis of Opportunity for Postsecondary Education: Oskaloosa, Iowa, November, 1997.

National Association for State Universities and Land Grant Colleges (NASULGC), Press Release: "New Commission to Bring Reform to State and Land-Grant Universities Funded by Kellogg Foundation." Washington, D.C. 30 January 1996.

Ohio State University Website (1999). OSU History.
   http://www.bet.ohio-state.edu/docs/osuhist.html

Our Ohio: A Digest of Facts About Ohio's History, Resources, Emblems and Famous People, 1970,
   State Historical Society of Wisconsin. PAM 76–617.

Pennsylvania's Ben Franklin Partnership. (1999.) http://www.benfranklin.org:80/

Peterson, Paul E. *The Price of Federalism.* Washington, D. C.: The Brookings Institution, 1995.

Pfeffer, Jeffrey. "Management as Symbolic Action: The Creation and Maintenance of
   Organizational Paradigms." In *Research in Organizational Behavior.* edited by L.
   Cummings and B. Staw, Vol. 3, No. 9, 21–48, (1981).

Pfeffer, Jeffrey and Gerald Salancik. (1978). "The Design and Management of Externally
   Controlled Organizations" In *The External Control of Organizations: A Resource
   Dependence Perspective*, New York: Harper-Row, 1978.

Reichardt, Charles S., and Sharon F. Rallis, (1994). "Qualitative and quantitative inquires are
   not incompatible: A call for a new partnership." In *The qualitative-quantitative
   debate: New perspectives*, edited by C.S. Reichardt & S. F. Rallis. San Francisco:
   Jossey-Bass, 1994.

Ruppert, Sandra. *The Politics of Remedy: State Legislative Views on Higher Education*. Littleton,
   CO: National Education Association, 1997.

Schein, Edgar H. *Organizational Culture and Leadership*. San Francisco: Jossey-Bass
   Publishers, 1992.

Schein, Edgar H. "The Learning Leader as a Cultural Manager." In, *Classic Readings in
   Organizational Behavior.* edited by J. S. Ott. New York: Harcourt Brace College
   Publishers, 1992.

Schuh, John H. "Fiscal Pressures on Higher Education and Student Affairs." In, *The
   Handbook of Student Affairs Administration*. San Francisco: Jossey-Bass Publishers,
   1993.

Scott, Richard W. *Organizations: Rational, Natural, and Open Systems*. Englewood Cliffs, NJ:
   Prentice Hall, 1992.

Schmidt, Peter. "Governors Want Fundamental Changes in Colleges, Question Place of
   Tenure." *Chronicle of Higher Education.* Vol. 44, No. 41, A38., (1998).

Scholtes, Peter R. *The Team Handbook for Educators: How to Use Teams to Improve Quality*.
   Madison, WI: Joiner Associates, Inc., 1994.

SPSS Base 8.0 User's Guide. Chicago, IL: SPSS, Inc., 1998.

Strang, William H., David L. Funk, and M. M. Onfornio. *Economic Impact of the University of
   Wisconsin System*. Madison, WI: University of Wisconsin-Madison, School of
   Business, 1997

Strauss, Anselm. and Juliet Corbin. *Basics of qualitative research: Grounded theory procedures and
   techniques*. Newbury Park, CA: Sage Publications, 1990.

Suchman, Mark. Lecture in Sociology Course #825: Complex Organizations. Madison, WI: University of Wisconsin-Madison, Fall, 1996

Tashakkori, Abbas and Charles Teddlie. *Mixed Methodology: Combining Qualitative and Quantitative Approaches.* London: Sage Publications, 1998.

Trombley, William. Higher Education Business Council: Virginia's coalition of business and academic leaders play political hardball. San Jose, CA: A report from the California Higher Education Policy Center. Vol. 5, No. 2. 1–10, 1997.

University of Georgia Website (1999). Brief History of UGA. www.uga.edu/uga/history.html

University of Wisconsin Foundation Website. (1999). *www.uwfound.wisc.edu*

University of Wisconsin-Madison Website (1999). UW-Madison History. www.wisc.edu

University of Wisconsin System Administration, (1999). 1999–2001 Biennial Budget Information. *www.uwsa.edu*

Van Maanen, John. "Reclaiming qualitative research methods for organizational research.." In *Qualitative Methodology* edited by J. Van Mannen. Beverly Hills, CA: Sage Publications, 1983.

Ward, David J. UW-Madison Chancellor David Ward Presentation to Educational Administration Course 940: Current Issues in Higher Education, Madison, WI., 26 April 1997.

Ward, David J. "The Challenges of Irreversible Change in Higher Education: The University of Wisconsin-Madison I n the 1990s." In, *Proud Traditions and Future Challenges: The University of Wisconsin-Madison Celebrates 150 Years.* edited by D. Ward and N. Radomski. Madison, WI: UW-Madison Office of University Publications, 1999.

Wildavsky, Aaron B. *The New Politics of the Budgetary Process.* HarperCollins Publishers: New York, 1992.

Index

www.ingramcontent.com/pod-product-compliance
Ingram Content Group UK Ltd.
Pitfield, Milton Keynes, MK11 3LW, UK
UKHW020417010325
455677UK00029B/920